Critics Praise K.V. Dominic's Verse

P C K Prem, renowned trilingual poet, novelist, short story writer, critic, as well as retired IAS officer from Himachal Pradesh, India is of opinion that K. V. Dominic's *Winged Reason* is a collection of poems of earthly imagination. Dominic's poetry is a document of social concerns in lyrics, beautiful and rhythmic. *Winged Reason* enshrines a definite message. Perhaps it is a rare collection of poems in Indian English Poetry that is realistic. Here, the words with the tonal values do not distract with multi-faceted meanings. The poet believes in simple, straight and plain language while showing genuine anxiety for socially neglected segments of society.

K. K. Srivastava, Indian Civil Servant as well as reputed English poet and critic in his review of *Winged Reason* states that the poems in this collection demonstrate a wide range of feelings from all walks of life. His poems are as close to nature as to human beings. He is a man who describes happiness & sorrow, plenty & poverty, rags & riches by placing them on equal footings. Some of his poems are philosophical in nature and describe the true characters of persons in modern society, touching the inmost chords of book lovers.

Chandramony Narayanaswami, English poet, short story writer and critic as well as retired IAS Officer from Odisha, India, in her assessment of *Write Son, Write* states that Prof. K. V. Dominic is a champion of peace and kindness to animals, in fact, all forms of life including plants and insects. One is tempted to describe him as the Buddha of the nuclear age. The first poem "Write My Son, Write" is a beautiful exposition of a poet's relevance in the modern age in which poetry has become the unwanted branch of literature. Enraged by the callousness, cruelty and sadism indulged in by men in general, the tortured Earth turns to the poet, the most sensitive being of the human race and coaxes him to write and inculcate the values of kindness, sensitivity, and refinement in the minds of his fellow beings.

Dr. A. K. Choudhary, Professor of English from Assam, India and a renowned English poet, critic and editor estimates that K. V. Dominic is the burning voice of Indian English poetry who has been perfuming the poetic scenario from a decade with his melodious song, fragrant feeling, racy style, capital ideas, and philosophical views. Dominic is the roaring voice of the creative milieu who has become a twinkling star in the sky of the creative world and has also been promoting the peeping poets for poetic perfection, prosperity, and peace. His forceful voice will remain ever ringing in the womb of time.

Winged Reason is the product of his mature wisdom and precious experiences. Social hypocrisy is under his targets of writing. Nature and her beauty, tsunami, men, women, god and proletariat are focused in detail. His poetic rosarium spreads iridescence across the literary world. Dominic's poetic style is also unrivalled. His poetic message covers all aspects of human lives and its problems. He is ever true to his words and conceptions. Man's deadly weapons pose a great threat to life itself. Man uproots millions of trees and exterminates thousands of animals. Capitalism rules the day. Equality has become utopian here. Women are sex instruments from birth to death. Her birth is considered a sign of ill omen. Dominic paints a lively picture of the workers who make castles and palaces but are prohibited from entering inside. He ridicules the hollowness of democracy while criminal MPs are brought from Jails to prove majority in the parliament. God is dethroned in the name of God. Human gods are crowned in the name of God.

Aju Mukhopadhyay, renowned Bilingual poet, critic, and essayist from Pondicherry, India, has reviewed K. V. Dominic's *Multicultural Symphony* and states that almost all his poems tell us that he never writes to express sheer beauty, passion for possession, spiritual aspiration or aesthetic pleasure. He is a realist with deep social feelings. Sufferings of any kind inflicted either by fate or man on man or animal make his heart bleed; loss of freedom suffocates him. With an empathic heart, he often sustains wounds at others' sufferings. But at some rare moments the nature lover in him appreciates nature's beauty and coming out, he peeps into a Cuckoo's nest.

K. V. Dominic
Essential Readings and Study Guide

Poems about Social Justice, Women's Rights, and the Environment

Edited by Victor R. Volkman

World Voices Series
Modern History Press
Ann Arbor • London • Sydney

K. V. Dominic Essential Readings and Study Guide: Poems about Social Justice, Women's Rights, and the Environment

Copyright © 2016 by K.V. Dominic. All Rights Reserved.

Learn more at www.profKVDominic.com

Edited by Victor R. Volkman

From the World Voices Series

Distributed by Ingram (USA/CAN/AU), Betram's Books (UK/EU)

ISBN-13: 978-1-61599-302-4 paperback

ISBN-13: 978-1-61599-303-1 hardcover

ISBN-13: 978-1-61599-304-8 eBook

Library of Congress Cataloging-in-Publication Data

Names: Dominic, K. V. (Kannappillil Varghese), 1956- | Dominic, K. V. (Kannappillil Varghese), 1956- author. Winged reason. | Dominic, K. V. (Kannappillil Varghese), 1956- author. Write son, write. | Dominic, K. V. (Kannappillil Varghese), 1956- author. Multicultural symphony.

Title: K. V. Dominic essential readings and study guide : poems about social
    justice, women's rights, and the environment / K. V. Dominic.

Other titles: Poems about social justice, women's rights, and the environment

Description: First edition. | Ann Arbor : Modern History Press ; Distributed
    by Ingram (USA/CAN/AU), Betram's Books (UK/EU), 2016. | Series: World
    voices series | Includes index.

Identifiers: LCCN 2016017238| ISBN 9781615993031 (hardcover : alk. paper) |
    ISBN 9781615993024 (pbk. : alk. paper)

Subjects: LCSH: Social justice--Poetry. | Women's rights--Poetry. | Environmentalism--Poetry. | Social problems--Poetry. | Social problems--Study and teaching.

Classification: LCC PR9499.4.D66 A6 2016 | DDC 821/.92--dc23

LC record available at https://lccn.loc.gov/2016017238

Published by	Tollfree (USA/CAN) 888-761-6268
Modern History Press	Fax 734-663-6861
5145 Pontiac Trail	www.ModernHistoryPress.com
Ann Arbor, MI 48105	info@ModernHistoryPress.com

Contents of Essential Readings

The *Essential Readings and Study Guide of K.V. Dominic* consists of three books previously published in India and a collection of previously unpublished works, now combined for the first time in this single volume. Each book has its own Table of Contents internal to itself and includes original front matter and poems. Scholars of K.V. Dominic have often pointed to the importance of insights revealed in Foreword and Introductions to these works.

Book 1 - Winged Reason	1
Book 2 - Write Son, Write	63
Book 3 -- Multicultural Symphony	141
Book 4 -- A Collection of New Poems	217
Evolution of a Poem: Siachen Tragedy	251
Index (Comprehensive)	256

WINGED REASON

K. V. DOMINIC

Dedicated to

My Beloved Father
Varghese Kannappilly

Contents:
Book 1 -- Winged Reason

Foreword	xi
Preface	xv
In Memoriam George Joson	1
Long Live E. K. Nayanar	3
A Blissful Voyage	5
A Nightmare	6
A Sheep's Wail	8
Anand's Lot	10
Beauty	12
Connubial Bliss	13
Cuckoo Singing	14
Gayatri's Solitude	15
Tsunami Camps	17
Harvest Feast	19
Haves and Have-nots	20
Helen and her World	22
I am Just a Mango Tree	24
International Women's Day	26
Lal Salaam to Labourers	28
Laxmi's Plea	30
My Teenage Hobby	32
Nature's Bounties	33
Old Age	35
Onam	37
Rahul's World	39
Sleepless Nights	40

Vrinda	41
What a Birth!	42
Human Brain	43
Indian Democracy	44
Ammini's Lament	46
Ammini's Demise	47
Om	49
Solar Eclipse	50
Pleasures and Pains	51
In the Name of God	52
City Versus Village	54
Cry of my Child	55
Kaumudi Teacher is no More	56
How I Became a Vegetarian	57
Michael Jackson, King of Kings	58
Synopsis	59
Reviews	60
About the Author	61

Foreword

Human mind is conditioned by experiences of and experiments with life. It is from mind that everything of imaginations, emotions, compassions, thoughts and revelations sprout. Poetry is output of all those which emanate from mind. I know Prof. K. V. Dominic personally and the poems included in this current collection, entitled *Winged Reason* are quite compatible with his mindset and mindscape. Prof. K. V. Dominic, a faculty member of the Post Graduate Department of English, Newman College, Thodupuzha, Kerala, India, and editor of the reputed biannual journal, *Indian Journal of Postcolonial Literatures,* is a sensitive and compassionate man whose sensitiveness and compassion are abundantly manifested in his poems. The following lines:

> I wish I had the claws of a vulture
> to fetch the skeletons from Iraq
> and build a bone-palace
> to imprison Bush in it.
>
> ("A Blissful Voyage")

demonstrate how much he is pained by Iraq war massacre. He is again pained to find plenty and poverty still staying together in our society:

> A wedding feast was served in the town hall,
> where expensive delicacies heaped on the plates.
> I could see two ragged girls outside
> struggling with the dogs in the garbage bin.
>
> ("A Nightmare")

Poet Dominic's perception of beauty is discernible in the line, "Eternal Beauty is in achievements eternal" ("Beauty").

Dominic describes the pathos of the modern cyber age civilisation, where children are sojourning to the opulent West, leaving old parents who are waiting for a phone call:

> looking at the far West,
> longing for her children's calls,
> she remains in solitude.
> How lucky were her parents!
> Lived happy, died happy;
> always with their children:
>
> ("Gayatri's Solitude")

This is a scenario of current loveless society.

Poet Dominic expresses anguish against man's unequal treatments towards fellowmen which plants and animals never do:

> Plants and animals never divide
> the earth among themselves;
> What right has the mortal man
> to divide and own this immortal planet?
>
> ("Haves and Have-nots")

Prof. Dominic's feeling for a sightless girl student in the classroom is affectionate and compassionate:

> She is the light of the class,
> light of the family,
> light of the village,
> but alas the light never sees itself.
>
> ("Helen and her World")

Dominic is a sympathetic and compassionate poet who is pained at humans' wanton felling of trees and destroying of nature's natural body ("I am Just a Mango Tree").

The poet's haikus on Nature's bounties are splendid:

> The Sun Kisses
> The eye opens
> Lotus blooms
>
> ("Nature's Bounties")

He is philosophic at other places also.

> The sun of knowledge
> can never be concealed
> by the moon of ignorance.
>
> ("Solar Eclipse")

Dominic has attempted to show how evils and sins are done by man in the name of God:

> God is dethroned
> in the name of God.
> And human gods are crowned
> in the name of God.
>
> ("In the Name of God")

Dominic's compassion, sympathy, philosophy are abundantly present in forty one poems in this collection.
In fine I should like to say:

He sang songs of his soul
which are compatible with
those of humanity whole.

> Pronab Kumar Majumdar
> (Former Secretary to the Govt. of W. Bengal)
> Poet, Playwright, Short Story Writer & Translator
> Editor: *Bridge-in-Making* (International Literary Journal)

Preface

Winged Reason is my maiden book of free verse consisting of thirty nine poems. It is the fruit of my five years of poetic voyage. Why the poetic muse eluded me till I was forty-eight was a question which my wife asked me recently and I am not able give a satisfactory reply. The reason might be that my life had gone smooth and comfortable without much itching of mind or arrows struck into it. As Jayanta Mahapatra wrote, poetry comes out of a "bad heart"—a heart that makes one turn secretly into a leader or a loser, pushing one to choose values, attitudes and do the not-so-obvious things ("Piercing the Rocks: Silence to Poetry"). I do believe that I matured very late, at the age of forty eight, to be able to choose values and impart them to my students as well as to the readers of my poems. Let me quote again Jayanta Mahapatra, who has been the greatest influence on my poetic musing:

> Poetry has always been responsible to life. By this, one means that a poet is first of all responsible to his or her own conscience; otherwise he or she cannot be called a poet. And may be the other factors necessary to the makings of a good poet, will only come later. These may ordinarily imply the craft, or the language the poet will use with skill in his poems. But somehow, these appear as frills in a poem that is already full with feeling, because the poem would have already done what it was meant to do; in other words, touch another human being, before one came to notice the other qualities of the poem.
> ("Piercing the Rocks: Silence to Poetry")

Let me make a criticism of my poems, as Seamus Heaney, the Nobel Laureate has always been doing to his poems. As a poet, I am responsible to my own conscience and I want to convey an emotion or a message often through social criticism. I have a commitment to my students as a professor; to the reader, scholars and writers as an editor; and to all human and non-human beings as a poet. Hence I give priority to the content of a poem than to the style of language. That is the reason why my poems lack much imagery and other figures of speech. I am of opinion that poetry should be digestible as short stories and novels are appealing to the ordinary laymen. I adopt conversational style in poetry, which again attracts the ordinary readers. Here I am influenced much by the Victorian poet, Robert Browning.

So the reason which my mind disallowed "robins" (a captivating image often used by my friend and great Indo/Canadian poet, Stephen

Gill) to enter and nest, is the security and comfort I enjoyed throughout my life. Stephen Gill has thus written in the preface to his masterpiece *The Flame*, "Discriminations and religious riots produced fears. They demolished whatever walls of security we had. These factors led me to the caves of isolation, thinking, browsing, and imagining that prepared a good recipe to be a poet" (14).

Compared to Stephen Gill's younger days in New Delhi, I have been living in this part of my country where there has been no communal riot or terrorist attack, and I have been positioned in the midst of plenty. Kerala, my State, is known outside as God's own land. There is equable climate; greeneries and natural beauties distinguish it from other States and tourist flood in from all parts of the world. Literacy is one hundred percent here and majority of the teenagers undergo education in schools and colleges. People here have a tendency to imitate the ways of the West, but unlike the Western people, the major concern of the people here is religion.

I have respect for Hinduism and Buddhism as they believe in Ahimsa. I feel remorse for having been a non vegetarian, eating meat and fish for fifty years. It is not an easy thing to change my staple when everyone around me dines with meat and fish. The death of my favourite twin cats haunts me every day and pricks my heart to bleed to new pastures of social criticism.

The world now shudders most because of terrorist attacks. Teenagers and youth are attracted to terrorism, mesmerized by the noble idea of self-sacrifices done to God. The antisocial leaders of terrorism exploit their religions to bring down the society to chaos, angst and panic. They loot the people, kidnap innocent persons and amass billions through bargain. The irony is that they do it in the name of God. When we go through the pages of world history we find that most of the homicides and genocides were done in the name of God.

Another thorn that thrusts my heart is the corruption done by the politicians and government officials. Poor people are strangled through taxes and their governments do nothing for their welfare. The government is always with the rich, caring for their comfort and luxury. The rich can evade taxes; exploit the weaker sections; torture and kill anyone they like; they get the protection of police; can escape legal punishments. Why because they have money. In fact my country as well as the world as such is ruled by a few multimillionaires who constitute not even one percent of the world population. It is a shocking truth that a thousand million people live in this world without a square meal a day when raw and cooked food in thousands of tons is wasted everyday. How can we justify this luxury? One can become rich only at the exploitation of the poor. It is the duty of the rich as well as the developed countries to alleviate the miseries of the poor.

The above mentioned are the arrows and thorns that pierce my heart everyday and the gushing blood runs through my pen to paper. Now, let me explain the immediate provocation which fired my imagination. One of my colleagues, Prof. George Joson, of the Department of Mathematics drowned in a river as he was driving back to his house at 11 pm on 14 May 2004. It was raining cats and dogs throughout the night, and the body was found out in the early morning frozen in the driver's seat of his car. Had there not been a flood in the river that night, he would not have died. Joson was my intimate friend, living with his unemployed wife and three little daughters—resembling three angels—just two hundred metres away from my house. Thus my "bad heart"—heavy and brimming with grief, released the tension on paper after two days.

The poetic muse--let me call it cuckoo, the bird which I like most—started to sing in my mind. Thank God, He sent the cuckoo to sit on the branch of my mind before it dried by old age. My first poem, "In Memoriam George Joson" was followed by "Long Live E. K. Nayanar." E. K. Nayanar, the Communist Chief Minister of Kerala died on 15th May 2004, the day when Joson's body was buried. Nayanar was the most lovable CM, Kerala had ever born. He was highly humourous, simple and as innocent as a lamb. Being a Socialist I have great love and respect for him. These two poems were published one after another in *Kerala Private College Teacher*, a journal of All Kerala Private College Teachers' Association and won acclaim from professors and lecturers in Kerala.

The popularity gained through the poems goaded me to write more and more and I tried my pen on various social issues. The major theme of my poetry is the eternal relationship between Man, Nature and God. Though baptized a Christian, I am primarily an Indian, and it is my duty as a teacher and poet to instil Indian values to my students and countrymen and also propagate these noble values to the rest of the world. I believe in the concept of jeevatma and paramatma (individual soul and universal soul) and that all living beings are part of paramatma or God. Again I believe in the Indian concept of Aham Brahmasmi (I am the God). Advaita seems to me more reasonable and acceptable than Dvaita. Thus I find the eternal affinity between Man, Nature and God. Man is not given liberty to kill other beings nor is he allowed to uproot plants and trees for his luxuries. The Creator has given man permission to use plants just for his survival. That is the law of Nature. No animal kills others except for food. Man needs only plants for his sustenance. His teeth and digestive system suit vegetarian diet. Adam and Eve lived on plants alone in the Garden of Eden. Animals were the close companions of our first parents. This philosophy of life is portrayed in several of my poems. "A Sheep's Wail," "Haves and Have-nots," "I am Just a Mango Tree," "My Teenage Hobby," "Ammini's Lament," "Ammini's Demise," "Om," "How I Became a Vegetarian," are the poems in this book proclaiming this theme.

Disparities in society, problems of the poor, the down-trodden, the marginalized and the old are the themes of the poems "A Nightmare," "Anand's Lot," "Beauty," "Tsunami Camps," "Gayatri's Solitude," "Helen and her World," "International Women's Day," "Lal Salaam to Labourers," "Laxmi's Plea," "Rahul's World," "Vrinda," "What a Birth!," "Cry of my Child," and "Old Age."

Politics, terrorism, communalism, corruption and exploitation by political parties and religions find subjects of thought in the poems "A Blissful Voyage," "God's will be Pleased," "Indian Democracy," "Solar Eclipse," and "In the Name of God."

Description of Nature is found in the poems "Nature's bounties," "Harvest Feast," "Cuckoo Singing," "Onam," and "Sleepless Nights."

In the poems "Kaumudi Teacher is no More" and "Michael Jackson, King of Kings," two celebrities in different fields are honoured.

The contrast of city and village lives is the theme of "City Versus Village." The ebb and flow of happiness and sorrow is the theme of the poem "Pleasures and Pains." In "Connubial Bliss" marriage is contrasted with celibacy. "Human Brain" is a poem drawing comparison of human brain with animal brain. Many of the poems in this book have been published periodically in national and international journals.

Now let me recollect the poets and philosophers who influenced my poetic musings. The Romantic poets--Wordsworth, Blake, Shelley and Keats fired my imagination considerably. The Victorians like Browning, Tennyson and Arnold and American poets Frost and Dickinson exercised their influence on me one way or other. Indian English poets, Ezekiel, Mahapatra and Kamala Das are my models in the use of diction and syntax. My own friends and contemporary poets, Stephen Gill, DC Chambial, PK Majumdar, Hazara Singh, OP Arora, Aju Mukhopadhyay, R. K. Bhusan, Jaydeep Sarangi, Sunil Sharma and several others contributed their share in my present development.

Christ, Vivekananda, Marx, Darwin, Sree Narayana, Said, Fanon, Gandhi, Nehru, Mother Teresa, Baba Amte, Salim Ali, Steve Irwin are the holy men, philosophers, theoreticians, humanitarians, ecologists and Nature lovers who shaped my view of life.

    I am winding up my preface with an acknowledgement to those who inspired me and helped me in the production of this book. First and foremost, my mind flies to Him with a bouquet of gratitude for allowing me to live all these years with a sound body and mind. I give Him special thanks for sending a cuckoo to my mind and making it sing continuously. Secondly I remember the inspiration given to me by my wife, Anne, and my children, Rose and Joe. They are also good critics of my poems. I am indebted to Prof. K. J. Francis, Nirmala College, Muvattupuzha, Kerala, who has been an admirer of my poems, and it was he who compelled me to publish this anthology. I am much obliged to my bosom friend, Mr. Sudarshan Kecherry, the proprietor of Authorspress, New Delhi, for accepting this book for publication. He is a rare gem among publishers—a scholar, a visionary, a sage and above all a proper guide to emerging writers. Finally I express my immense gratitude to my former student, Mr. K. K. Anas, Research Scholar in France, for the wonderful illustrations and cover design of this book.

K. V. Dominic

In Memoriam George Joson

(elegy written on a colleague who died
in a car accident on 14. 05. 2004)

Why did you leave us so soon, dear Joson?
(We are unable to find any reason.)
It stunned and benumbed us.
How unbearable the grief and pain
For your beloved family and friends
The most painful was the sight
When your youngest kid,
not knowing what has happened,
kissed your face often
and plucked flowers
from your wreath;
tossed them to her sisters weeping and screaming
What a game He plays!
When He comes with His chariot,
none can say--"wait".
Joson
Now we understand the mystery of your ever being fast--
fast in your words;
fast in your walk;
fast in your action,
and FAST UNTO DEATH.
Life is uncertain
for the mighty and the meek
grants it certainty
Also to those
who are our charge
And deny them the risk of fall--
Great is the loss
to academia too.
Your absence, everywhere is haunting
We find it hard
to console and reconcile
with the inevitable!
We are all
bound by His will

to be here
to be away.
As the great poet sang:
We are all puppets in His hands,
dancing to His various tunes.
The best is to resign
to what He ordains
in time and out of time.

Questions

- What is the attitude of the poet to Death?
- Who is the great poet meant in the lines: "We are all puppets in His hands, / dancing to His various tunes"?

Long Live E. K. Nayanar

(elegy written on E. K. Nayanar*
who passed away on 15. 05. 2004)

"Long live E. K. Nayanar!"
This mantra is being muttered
by millions of your comrades.
We are in a trance
since you bade us "Good bye."
It is impossible to believe
our dearest CM is no more.
A vast surging
sea of humanity
followed wailing and weeping
on your last journey.
No rain could stop them;
no sleep could retreat them.
Thus mourning with the Nature,
your people swarmed round your body,
bidding "Lal Salaam, Lal Salaam.'
You were a true Communist;
a comrade to the core of your being,
a rare species,
compassion and love
an epitome of Socialism.
Yet did give due respect and valued
those even who differed from you.
Your rhetoric left a lasting spell!
your utterances dance
on the tongues and lips of your sheep.
Deep sounding like a bassoon,
it stirred and the public cheered.
Was it mere rhetoric
that enchanted your audience?
Nay, the words came from your heart;
you meant what you spoke.
people believed
what you said.

Such was your charisma;
It reminds us of the rare species
of rhetoricians and statesmen.
You were truly a patriot;
had no foes, only friends.
Your heart bled at the sight of
the tears of the poor,
the miseries of the wretched,
the sufferings of the downtrodden,
pricked your heart often.
You championed the cause of the denied
and the deprived.
your sense of humour was inimitable
very few leaders sparkled in that.
Your absence from amidst us
shows your presence among the stars.
You are our polestar
who saves us from the Darkness.
You will continue to steer
the ship of our dear nation
to the land of the blessings and bounties.

E. K. Nayanar: Thrice Chief Minister of Kerala, India

Questions

- What are the qualities that made Chief Minister E. K. Nayanar favourite of the people?

A Blissful Voyage

Let my mind soar high
on the wings of the Muses
and visit the places
inaccessible.

Had I the wings of a mallard
I could fly to the States,
shake the hand of Obama,
and thank my American sisters and brothers.

I wish I had the claws of a vulture
to fetch the skeletons from Iraq
and build a bone-palace
to imprison Bush in it.

If I could fly like an angel,
would plead all prophets
to inspire and instil humanism
in millions' communal minds.
I would meet Gandhi too
who is weeping at his shattered dreams.

I wish I were a bullet
and shoot into the chest of that terrorist
who compels that teen age boy
to explode and kill that innocent mob.

Questions
- What are the imageries used in the poem?
- What is poet's reaction to terrorism?

A Nightmare

I had a nightmare the overnight;
I was a hawk hovering in the sky.

I could view the cry of an obese boy
whose mother was beating him to eat more.
A cry of a different note was heard from the next door,
where a bony child was crying for a crumb.

A lavish wedding feast was served in the town hall,
rich delicacies heaped on the plates,
were relished by the pompous guests
I could see two ragged girls outside
struggling with the dogs in the garbage bin.

My wings took me to a public school;
A boy in tears stood on the veranda:
A punishment for not wearing his tie!
In the humid weather of forty degree
a slavish mimic, a legacy of the West.

What's that long queue I find before that shop?
Like a line of ants before their hole.
God! It's a liquor shop run by the government!
That leper who begged at my door is also in the line!
A similar queue is found on the other side,
where poor women wait for their rations.

Then I found a public water tap
that made the road a black river.
Elsewhere I noticed a waterless tap
laughing at the hopeless wait
of all the pots of the neighbourhood.

See, what a mansion that double-storied edifice!
Luxury rooms, lawn and swimming pool;
An old man and his wife resided there;
sitting at the phone with sighs and moans,
longed for the calls from their sons abroad.

Not far away were the slums of the city;
three generations lived in each hut;
grandpa, grandma, their sons and their wives,
and their little kids sleep in a room!

Tears streamed down my cheeks
I could see nothing more;
nor did I wish for it;
The siren sounded as usual
to disturb my nightmare.

Questions
- Which are the antitheses used in this poem?

A Sheep's Wail

Hark, you Man
to my wail,
your enslaved sheep's.

You are possessed with
some special powers
that we do not have.

With your brain
and with your tongue
you conquered us.

superior you boast,
but inferior you become
to the microbes that kill you.

The fur God gave me,
mercilessly you shear
to make you cosy.

The milk for my lamb
you suck and drain
and grow fat and cruel.

I have seen with my eyes
and heard with my ears
the last cries of my parents.

When they became old
you cut their heads
and ate their flesh.

Man, you are the cruellest,
you are the most ungrateful
of all God's creations.

Yet you find justification
and bring false philosophies

to make you His choicest.

Nothing can be more absurd!
Aren't we His children?
How can He forgive you?

If a heaven is there
we will reach there first
and pray to God to shut you out.

Questions

- Why is Man called the cruellest and ungrateful of God's creations?
- Why does the sheep think that if a heaven is there it will reach there first?

Anand's Lot

Anand's eyes were immersed
on the pupils in tempting uniforms;
compared with his shabby ragged dress.
Longed to be one of them again.
How happy were those days!
Mummy gave me kiss and ta-ta;
like butterflies flew to the school
with Rajesh, Praveen and Smitha
chattering, singing, dancing, running.
Alas! Like a vulture came the car then;
picked me in and dashed away.
A bearded-man with a black towel
hushed my helpless wail for help;
brought into a house and shut in a room.
I was fed with cold dry bread
and slept on the floor dead tired.
The car picked me again in the morning
and brought me to this strange city.
They changed my dress
and dressed me in rags.
They threatened to kill me
if I disobeyed their orders.
I have to sleep in their hut,
eat dry bread which I hate;
always wear this stinky rags.
They scold me and beat me
for not earning much as they dreamed.
Many months have passed
since I left my mummy, dad and Smitha?
Are they still crying at my loss?
Tears streamed down from Anand's cheeks.
"Bloody dog, why are you standing still?"
The bearded-man slapped helpless Anand.
"Go to the shops and beg or I'll kill you."
Crying, Anand stretched his hand
went begging shop after shop.

Questions
- What is Anand's fate?

Beauty

Why do you murmur lass looking at the mirror?
Ma, why didn't God create me a little more beautiful?
Who told you dear that you are not beautiful?
Bodily beauty is only one among the beauties;
It fades and decays as a flower does.
Who thinks of a flower when it is decayed?
The sun is beautiful but can you enjoy it at noon?
The objects of nature reveal its radiance and beauty.
Eternal beauty is in achievements eternal.
Handsome is he who handsome does.
So it is said.
look and think of
Gandhi, Lincoln, Shakespeare, Shaw,
Mother Teresa, Navratilova, Venus, Sereena…
Who is more popular, Venus or Aiswarya?
What makes Kalam our dearest President?
Bodily beauty is all subjective and relative;
Some like white, some like black.
No child is ugly to its mother;
Nothing can be ugly, for God created it.
Didn't you feel the snake's beauty
when Lawrence sang in praise of it?
Keats has taught you "beauty is truth"
and "a thing of beauty is a joy for ever."
Only spiritual beauty gives eternal joy.
My dear lass, be like the sun,
brightening this dark world with your inner beauty.

Questions

- What message does the poet convey through the poem?
- What is the title of D. H. Lawrence's poem on snakes?

Connubial Bliss

Proton, electron; positive, negative;
male, female; made for each other.
Pains and pleasures: God's own gifts.
None can reject them.

Divine sex, divine organs;
instincts divine, divine pleasures;
who can abstain them?

The dancing of the plant;
the smiling of the flower;
the chirping of the bird;
and all merry cries of other beings,
herald Life's march here.

Connubial bliss,
heavenly happiness;
merging of two souls;
fulfilment of His plans.

Questions
- Why does the poet level connubial bliss to heavenly happiness?

Cuckoo Singing

4.30 a.m.
Cuckoos' songs echo:
waking call
for dreaming day.
Sweetest song in Nature;
sweeter than any
man-made music;
Orpheus, Beethoven,
none before it.
Ku, ku, khu, khhu, khhoo;
the note goes
up and up and up and up.
What do the sounds mean?
"Wake up mate,
let's start love" or
"Wake up man and
sweat for your bread"?
Yes, cuckoo lives
singing and loving,
while man exists
sweating and moaning

Questions

- What is the difference between cuckoo's life and man's life?
- What is the figure of speech used in the phrase "Cuckoos' song echo"?

Gayatri's Solitude

Gayatri aged eighty two,
widowed at thirty five,
mother of five children:
three sons and two daughters;
all in the States.
Old-age home her haven.
The palatial house
her children built
remains empty at town.
Her room in old-age home
modern with AC.
She will get any food;
all left to her choice.
Her children under illusion:
their mother is cosy.
Poor, miserable mother,
she has no hunger,
she has no sleep.
An old lily flower
pale and faded.
Dawn to dusk,
sitting in an armchair,
looking at the far West,
longing for her children's calls,
she remains in solitude.
How lucky were her parents!
Lived happy, died happy;
always with their children:
sons, daughters,
daughters-in-law,
sons-in-law,
a dozen grand children,
a house full of mirth.
The depth of maternal love,
and the pangs of separation
no child can gauge.

Questions
- What is the theme of the poem?
- What is the reason for Gayatri's solitude?

Tsunami Camps

How dreadful the life in Tsunami camps!
People burnt in man-made hells;
gods crazy seeing their sufferings.
Months have passed
since Tsunami tossed them from their houses.
Nothing left but mind and body;
counting days for their salvation.
Lost their dear ones
and fight against destiny.
Camps built of GI sheet
melt inmates trapped in the cells.
A furnace inside, a furnace outside;
mind and body burn with agony.
Each family has a cell in the camp;
they cook and dine and sleep at night;
grown-ups sleep outside, risking nightly rains.
Government gave kits and boxes;
kits don't contain essential things;
hearth produces smoke than flames.
None hears their cries and complaints:
"Where have gone the crores
collected for our relief?"
Money is hoarded in the government exchequer,
or diverted for some other purposes.
"It's better to kill us than torture like this."
"We don't have sufficient food,
we don't have pure water."
"The filthy atmosphere of the camp
will bring several epidemics."
"Give us boats and nets,
and we will earn our livelihood."
"We don't get any help
either from the Right or from the Left."
Unending wails and unending sobs;
not even gods listen to their cries.

Questions
- What is meant by the phrase "A furnace inside, a furnace outside"?
- What are the complaints of the Tsunami victims in the camps?

Harvest Feast

That photograph in the newspaper
flashes to my mind very often;
Those little pupils from Kozhikode,
avidly feasting rice and payasam;
The harvest banquet of their sweated labour.
Nothing can be tastier than this.

Those nimble, soft feet,
which ran after butterflies;
Those little velvety hands
which caressed plants and flowers,
moved through the rough fields;
ploughed the land; sowed the seed;
plucked the weed; reaped the corn;
carried sheaves on their tender heads;
threshed, husked, cooked.

Their teachers taught them the great lessons:
how education can be vocational;
and the beauty and dignity of labour;
a lesson too to the adult world:
the way to solve the food crisis,
and save the world from poverty.

Questions
- What are the great lessons that the teachers taught their pupils?
- Why is the pupils' harvest feast tastier than all other feasts?

Haves and Have-nots

Haves and Have-nots:
man-made categories;
never in creator's dream.

Abundant Nature
feeds plants and animals.
Greedy selfish man disrupts
Mother Nature's feeding;
uproots millions of trees,
exterminates thousands of animals.
His deadly weapons
pose great threat
to life itself.

Man is a wonderful work;
Unimaginable his achievements;
Equally heart-rending his destructions.
Achievements prove beneficial
only to Haves a minority.

When millions die of hunger,
thousands compete for delicacies.
Minority always luxuriates
at the cost of
majorities' necessities.

Plants and animals never divide
the earth among themselves;
What right has the mortal man
to divide and own this immortal planet?
What justice is there for the minority
to starve the majority to death?

How pitiable
that religions give no solace and hope
to the miserable multitudes.

The Have-nots found a haven
in socialism and communism;
no private property;
state-owned wealth;
selfless work for the society.
But power corrupted;
leaders turned tyrants;
philosophy failed.
Equality to man utopian.

Capitalism rules the day;
Have-nots numbers swell.
Shattered and smashed
are their dreams
of health and happiness.

Questions

- Is the division between Haves and Have-nots justifiable? Explain.
- Why does the poet think that the Have-nots number will increase in future?

Helen and her World

Helen, her restless eyes
pierce my heart very often;
Those lovely eyes of hers,
searching for a ray of light
from the very first day
she came to this world:
a world without
the sun and the moon;
prick my heart and
it bleeds in the class.

The analogy of the lamp and the pot
I lectured for the Rasa theory;
how the lamp reveals the pot;
sparkled the eyes of others,
while her eyes were still
searching for the lamp and its light.

When she takes down notes,
faster than any typewriter,
ticked, ticked moves her hand
line after line on the Braille;
as I speed to her ticks
others struggle to keep her pace.

She is the brightest in the class;
reads books after books
through her brother's eyes.
Had her scribe known
spelling of all her words,
she could have won a rank
in her degree examinations.

She is the light of the class,
light of the family,
light of the village,
but alas the light never sees itself,
and of course

light shows all
their path and ways
and can't see itself!
What is challenge to the challenged!
Light fighting against darkness,
Eternally! Hopefully! Surely!
Helen is comfortable in life.

Questions

- What is the message of the poem?
- What irony do you find in the poem?

I am Just a Mango Tree

I am just a Mango Tree;
still an accomplished life;
I've fulfilled my Creator's plan.
Standing like a Himalayan umbrella,
I shelter my student-friends
waiting for the buses.
The Sun can't wither them,
nor Rain wets them.
Their innocent smiles and laughter;
the lovers sighs and sobs,
tickle me or weep me.
When my friend the Wind comes,
I welcome him with myriad hands.
My saviour Sun fosters me;
his rays cook food for me;
I grow and bear fruits for others.
When I blossom, flies kiss me.
My branches are the beds for birds;
cuckoos, crows and mynahs come;
when my fruits are ripe, a feast to them.
Their chirps and songs lull me often;
when night comes they sleep on my lap;
I too sleep standing on my feet.
Nightly breeze and dews caress me;
I drop mellow yellow fruits
to my beggar friend who sleeps beneath.
My God, how happy I feel—
The fruit of service!
Hark! What's that boy telling the girl?
"Darling, where shall we wait
when they cut this tree?"
"Dear, why do they cut this tree,
a harbour to hundreds of us?"
"They plan to build a waiting shed here."
God, what do I hear? Is it true?
'True, my daughter, I am helpless.'
Can't they spare me and
build it somewhere else?

Don't I do them good as to all?
Don't I have feelings and pains
though I endure in silence?
Haven't I the right to live?
God, why is your Man so selfish and cruel?
Did you create him,
to disturb this earth's balance?
This planet would be a paradise
if you kindly withdraw him.
'My child, I created him
in My own image
but he's gone astray;
My agony is endless.
That's the fate
of the father everywhere.
I shouldn't have created this human species;
But how can a father kill his sons?'

Questions

- What is the theme of the poem?
- How does Man disturb earth's balance?

International Women's Day

(Composed on 8 March 2009)

International Women's Day;
celebrations all over the world;
meetings held;
programmes chalked out;
promises showered;
fund allotted;
celebrities honoured;
her praises sung hoarse
coarse in her life's course
mockery's rhetoric in these celebrations!
All echoes of years of yore.
Problems remain the same!
Woman is the game!
Birth to death,
an instrument of lust
and hot-selling sex.
Her very birth ill omen:
an unwelcome event.
No guilt in foeticide;
foeticide is matricide;
no life without mother.
Sexism in childhood;
priority to her brother;
her food, his leftover.
Chained in kitchen,
she rarely goes out.
No toys, no plays;
always envies him.
Mum and dad love him;
she gets only reproaches;
beat her very often.
Seldom educated;
hence no employment,
and always dependant.
No choice of her partner;

her individuality
scantily respected.
Born to be dictated;
tyranny everywhere:
slave to her husband,
servant to her in-laws.
Bears the burden of birth;
lives for her children.
Dawn to dusk,
blood turns sweat.
Her love never returned.
Has no place in politics:
councils, assemblies, parliaments,
she has little or unheard voice.
Religions also dishonour her:
she has no right
to enter her Father's abode;
no place in clergy.
She is always the Other.
Patriarchy is his product;
he dictates the world;
dictates even God,
and corrupts religion.
He writes scriptures,
makes sexism predestinate.
Venerable is woman,
for she is your mother;
she is you sister;
she is your wife;
she is your guide;
she is your teacher;
she is your nurse;
and above all,
she is your angel.

Questions

- What are the problems, hardships and discriminations faced by women?
- Why does the poet say that woman is venerable?

Lal Salaam to Labourers

Lal Salaam to Labourers,
the backbone of the country!

They sow the seed;
reap the corn;
and we eat and sleep.

They spin and weave;
make beautiful clothes;
and we wear and 'shine.'

They build houses
where they never rest,
and there we live and snore.

They sweat in factories;
produce numberless goods;
and we use and enjoy.

They tar the road;
melt in the furnace;
and we ride and drive.

They clean roads and markets;
are shunned by us very often;
and we make them filthier and filthier.

They envy our lives;
nurse bubbles of dreams;
but reality pricks them of,
and many find haven in tavern.

Lal Salaam to Labourers,
for without them we have no life.

Let us not be stingy
when we pay them wages,
for we can't do what they do.

Give them at least their due;
the more we give, the more we get;
Put charity in humanity
a spiritual bliss that never dies.

Questions

- What are the major services of the labourers portrayed in the poem?
- Why do many labourers find a haven in tavern?

Laxmi's Plea

Rekha's wedding today;
my youngest colleague
junior by ten years.
To be or not to be;
present or absent;
a terrible trance!
Auspicious occasion;
jocund jolly hall;
a fish out of water;
I can't slither there.
"Laxmi, when is your wedding?"
"Laxmi, you alone remain."
Can't bear these arrows;
heart full of such arrows;
bleeding day after day.
It's none my fault
single at thirty three.
"Laxmi looks very handsome."
"She is a lamp to any house."
A lamp destined to burn out
under a hot pot.
Plenty of proposals;
appeared with tea
before many young men.
None complained my looks.
"What's the dowry?"
A stumbling block to all proposals.
Father died when I was ten;
mother bed-ridden with cancer;
a thatched house in five cents;
an elder sister married off.
My meagre salary two thousand
hardly meets our food and medicine.
I have pricked my bubble of dreams;
let none dream for me.
Leave me alone;
leave me single.

Questions
- What is the theme of the poem?
- What is Laxmi's plea to the world?

My Teenage Hobby

Angling, my teenage hobby;
evenings at river bank
with Joseph till early night.
Long wait for the catch;
amidst mosquitoes.
Each fish a great thrill;
pulling the fish out of water:
a heavenly experience!
The death struggle
of the innocent fish.
Sadistic pleasure!
Once when I pulled a fish,
flashed a horrible vision:
I am pulled from the sky;
death struggle on the line.
Awestruck and repentant,
I unhooked the fish
and dropped in the water.
No more did I angle;
Reflections on life
became my pastime.

Questions
- Why did the poet stop his hobby of angling?

Nature's Bounties

(Haiku sets)

The song of cuckoo
Night's dirge
Day's trumpet

The birth of morn
Temples and mosques chanting hymns
Heaven on earth

The sun kisses
The eye opens
Lotus blooms

Fragrance of the rose
Intoxication to the fly
Dancing round the plant

Jasmine's hand
Caressing touch on my neck
Utter dilemma

Mellow yellow papaya
Longing violent kisses
Feasting to crows and mynahs

Lightning and thunder
God's fire works
Frightened man quirks!

Torrential summer rains
A shed of corrugated sheets
God's drum beats!

Parched fields
Rain in summer
Honey to the lips

Refreshing downpour
A child in ecstasy
Drenched dancing

Road a river of rainwater
A child on bicycle
Splashing roaring

Snow-capped mountain
Multi-coloured sky
God with the brush

Questions
- What is a haiku?
- What is the dilemma of the poet when jasmine's hand touches his neck?

Old Age

Human life is a cycle:
born to the earth
with a shrieking cry;
life's first breath.
Bed-ridden first year,
dependent childhood,
independent youth;
gives birth to children;
health wanes;
dependent old age;
body week;
but mind strong;
bed-ridden at last;
lies back to the earth
with a painful breath.
Childhood is memorable—
carefree and dynamic
no sorrow dares
but happiness glares.
one with Nature;
an angel on earth;
daring to all.
Old age begins to play its colours—
The monarch of yesterday,
feels humbled today.
Imprisoned amidst unripe ripeness;
utterly helpless.
unyielding mind.
The dearest children
to whom he looked and loved
turn ungrateful.
They hate and curse
And never care.
Ageism is contemptible;
unpardonable too.
Today's torturer
tomorrow's victim;
we live with ironies.

Questions
- How is human life a *cycle*?
- How does today's torturer become tomorrow's victim?

Onam

Onam, a national festival;
Keralites celebrate
wherever they are.
Ten days celebrations
starting with Atham:
a harvest festival.
Feasting with new rice
after three months of
continuous monsoon.
Clear sky and bright sunlight;
fragrance and colours
of flowers everywhere.
Early mornings
children run for flowers,
make pookalams
at the front yards.
Pookalams with
myriads of flowers
in circular pattern:
a fantastic sight!
People in new dress;
full of gaiety and spirits;
relishing ceremonial food;
delight in Onam songs,
Onam plays and Onam dances.
Spirited competitions:
sports, games and arts;
a familiar sight.
Boat races with
dozens of rowers
in bright uniforms,
rowing in perfect rhythm,
singing boat songs,
a pageant rare beauty in the world.
Onam has a legend:
a remembrance of
the golden rule of Maveli
an icon of the just king.

Equality prevailed in society;
no lies, no crimes, no deceits;
and no cheat;
no poverty, no child death.
All were happy;
heaven cannot be different!
Envious of Maveli
Vishnu in disguise
stamped on his head
to be thrown in the underworld.
But granted him a boon
to visit his people
once in a year.
Maveli visits on Onam;
Fed up,
he returns in tears.

Keralites: People of Kerala, the southern state of India. Known as God's own land it has pleasant, equable climate and high density of population. Full of natural beauties it is dear to the foreign tourists.

Pookalams: Flower designs

Vishnu: One of the trinities of Hindu religion.

Questions

- Why does Maveli return in tears?

Rahul's World

"Rahul, get out,"
teacher roared,
class shuddered.
Rahul wept,
stood outside.

Couldn't study
yesterday's portion.
Whose fault?

Drunken father
beat mother,
beat Rahul;
kicked away supper,
none could sleep.

Cruel father,
Cruel teacher,
Cruel world,
Poor Rahul
longs for love.

Questions

- Why couldn't Rahul study previous day's portions?

Sleepless Nights

The Cuckoo's flute
woke me up at every dawn;
but lately having little sleep,
I lie restless for hours and hours,
longing vainly to wake him up.

The Cuckoo lies on his God-given bed;
the gentle breeze always caresses him;
the nocturnal music lulls him throughout,
and his sleep is sound
free from cares and worries.

I lie in my concrete house,
fighting against the man-made heat,
and the dreary sound of the hot-wave fan.
The late and heavy supper in stomach,
and all such unnatural ways of life
take away that God's own gift.

Ah, the Cuckoo finally calls me out;
let me get up, get out of my cell,
and have a bath in the pool of morning beauty.

Questions
- How is the poet's night different from cuckoo's night?
- Why does cuckoo have a sound sleep?

Vrinda

Vrinda, twelve or thirteen
on the TV yesterday.
angelic her appearance,
dancing like a peacock
to Hindi film tunes.
Ha! Dancing just on one leg.
The other leg?
Folded under skirt?
Eyes searched for it.
God, only one leg!
Skipping like kangaroo.
Pricked my heart;
started aching.
Why is destiny so cruel?
She illumines this world;
entertains millions.
Who can console her?
Who will please her?
Her life only begun;
has suffered much.
Thousands of miles ahead
to tread with lone leg.
She turned her challenge
to strength and success.
A loud message for the world!

Questions
- What message does Vrinda give to the world?

What a Birth!

Just returned
from the furnace
after the tarring work.

Burning body
longing cooling haven
but a frozen house.

A thatched hut
cardboard walls
boltless door.

Bed-ridden mother
hungry mouth
beckoning me.

Daughter from school
empty stomach
longing for food.

Rice in the pot
lunch for ma and daughter
stray dogs feasted.

Drunkard husband
will come at night
to resume beats and kicks.

Dawn for doom
Dusk to damn
What a birth!

Questions
- Who is the protagonist of the poem?
- What is the theme of the poem?

Human Brain

Human brain;
the centre of
pleasures and pains;
that which makes man
distinct from other beings;
a boon or bane?
Birds of the sky;
all beings of the land;
fishes in water;
past never haunts,
nor their future.
No worries;
no dreams;
content always.
If heaven is happiness,
and happiness heaven,
they are in
and we are out.

Questions

- Why is the poet sceptical about the human brain?
- Why does the poet say that non-humans will enter heaven but humans won't?

Indian Democracy

Indian democracy:
the largest on the planet;
a wonder to the world.
Parliament elections:
several billions business;
stage of heinous means.
Secularism butchered;
caste and religion
raise their hood;
regionalism and parochialism
devour
nationalism and patriotism.
National parties play
trump cards with communalism;
bow their heads before priests.
The real issues of the country
never discussed among people.
Election campaigns:
fireworks of lies and abuses.
Terrorists try to sabotage,
killing civilians, police, soldiers.
Thus democracy reigns
drinking tears of thousands!
Criminal MPs,
brought from jails
to prove majority on floor;
horse-trade of billions!
Corrupt governments,
draining the blood of people.
Gratitude to the voters!
Gullible people,
they vote them again and again;
no other options.
Still democracy shall prevail
or tyranny will
sit on the Chair.

Questions

- What are the defects the poet points out of the Indian democracy?
- Why does the poet say that the democracy shall prevail?

Ammini's Lament

How to expiate
the merciless sin
committed to my cat?
Ammini's heart-broken wails,
her unnatural reverberating cry,
shooting like arrows
through my heart,
and then to my wife.
Ammini can't forget
even after ten days
the loss of her darlings.
Day in and day out
she wanders on all sides
seeking the twins of her triplet.
When troubles increased,
in a weak moment
I had to sell them.
Ammini's incessant cry,
like Gandhari's wails,
echoes my premises.
The pangs of my heart,
a laughingstock to my guests;
Inhumane to animals,
they do believe,
all creations are for men,
since they are born
in God's own image.
Ammini's changed a lot;
no greed for food;
no frolic with her son.
How long will she go on wailing?
Will she curse me as Gandhari did?
Destined like the 'Ancient Mariner'
I'm desperate for the purging amends.

Questions

- What is the reason for Ammini's lament?

Ammini's Demise

My Ammini cat's demise
steals my sleep.
Day in day out,
her snow white figure,
her emerald eyes,
black bushy tail,
her gentle demeanour,
her sleep on my lap,
throng my heart,
and hangs me down.
Let me add to Keats':
A thing of beauty
is a joy for ever;
and its loss
is sorrow for ever.
Poisoned to death
Ammini's struggle
for breath and water;
our effort in vain
to keep her alive;
and her final adieu
without even a sound;
wife's moans and wails,
haunt me and
my mind bleeds,
pricked by thorns around.
God, why did you
call her back?
Lived only one year;
gave only happiness.
She was a friend
to my lonely mother;
gave solace to her
when gasping for breath.
How could that fiend
poison this angel?
What harm had it
done to him?

When he was sleeping sound
my darling was
struggling for breath.
Thousands of fiends
inhabit this planet,
turning the earth
to a big slaughter house,
as if man alone has
 the right to live here.
God, make them humane
and turn them into angels.

Questions

- How did Ammini die?
- How did Ammini's demise affect the poet and his family?

Om

Om, the birth-cry of this world;
the very first sound echoing everywhere;
the rhythm of all creations;
from atoms to stars
Om goes on ringing.
Combination of three letters,
representing Vishnu, Shiva, Brahma,
and meaning Brahman.
Father of all mantras;
past and future live in this sound.
Once monopoly of the high caste;
low-caste people were denied
it's listening and muttering;
destined to recite 'On.'
Worm-like man challenges the Creator;
Om, the holiest mantra of mantras;
key to all problems of the world;
Om is our breath;
a tonic to mind and body.
It's a celestial music
showering manna on the earth;
it gives us peace and happiness;
Om shanty, Om shanty, Om shanty.

Questions
- What are the characteristics and powers of Om?

Solar Eclipse

The moon tried hard
to hide the sun;
but the radiant brilliance
spilled over the moon.
Humiliated and frightened
she slid from his presence.

The sun of knowledge
can never be concealed
by the moon of ignorance.

Moons of the world here
seduce suns of virtue.
Corrupt governments devour
suns of innocence.
Fair is foul here
and foul is fair.

Questions

- What message does the poet bring out through the imagery of solar eclipse?
- Why does the poet say that *fair is foul here and foul is fair*?
- What other writer first used these lines?

Pleasures and Pains

Pleasures and pains:
two sides of a coin.
We toss it early morning;
majority gets the pains side.
Pleasures come like sprinkle,
while pains fall like deluge
and continue like monsoon.
Happiness is a mist
while sorrows shower like snow.

Questions
- How is pleasures and pains contrasted by the poet?

In the Name of God

Criminal actions done
in the name of God
outnumber
philanthropic services done
in the name of God.
Millions were killed in crusades
in the name of God.
Tens of millions died in World Wars
in the name of God.
Clergies thrive and dictate
in the name of God.
Laymen frightened surrender
in the name of God.
Religions rival each other
in the name of God.
Democracy is devalued
in the name of God.
Nepotism is supported
in the name of God.
Superstitions survive
in the name of God.
Communalism poisons
in the name of God.
Communism is strangled
in the name of God.
Terrorists butcher thousands
in the name of God.
Teens become terrorists
in the name of God.
Sexism prevails
in the name of God.
Higher castes exploit
in the name of God.
Secularism is nullified
in the name of God.
Corruption is promoted
in the name of God.
God is dethroned

in the name of God.
And human gods are crowned
in the name of God.

Questions

- What is the theme of the poem?
- List some unholy things and criminal actions done in the name of God.

City Versus Village

"Dear, it seems some neighbour is dead."
"Yea, the dirge is from a close house.
Just go and seek," my wife said.
The mournful song
came from a rented house.
Though near by a hundred metres,
we never went there,
nor they visited our house.
The head of the house lay dead
in a flower covered freezer.
While alive might have dreamed
of an AC bed room.
Alas, he got it with high interest;
his body shrunken to the bones.
an insult to the dead!
I join the mourning with
the bereaved family,
though none is known to me.
How hard it is--
the city dwellers--
Busy and selfish.
devoid of humanity
Each one lost
in his own island.
A crow, friendly to community;
A dog there is
friendly to other dogs.
How innocent and malice-free
is village life
where all live
in harmony and love.
They are gullible--
so fooled and cheated
and looted by the townsmen.

Questions

- Bring out the contrast between city life and village life.

Cry of my Child

God, can't bear that
heart-rending cry,
piercing like an arrow
through my heart.
She is hungry
and needs feeding;
breasts are swelling with milk.
How will I complete the exam?
Two more hours left;
easy questions;
know all answers;
but can't concentrate;
the pen isn't moving.
Graduate and unemployed;
took my BA five years back;
applied for many jobs;
wrote tests after tests.
Husband daily labourer;
sole earner of the family;
has to feed seven members;
his aged parents
and his younger sisters.
Oh, my child is still crying;
sister-in-law is helpless.
Should I quit and feed my child?
God, don't you hear my cry?

Questions

- What miserable problem of Kerala is pointed out in the poem?

Kaumudi Teacher is no More

Kaumudi Teacher is no more with us;
that light has gone out on fourth August.
The beacon which guided many women
was destroyed by the wave of Time.
A lone fighter, a role model;
A single woman to fulfil her mission.
Driven by her father's vision,
joined Congress in her teen age.
Gandhi's charisma drew her like a magnet;
attended Gandhi's address at Vadakara;
A meeting to raise fund for Harijan.
Exhorted men and women to be generous;
women might donate their ornaments.
Kaumudi, only sixteen, mounted the stage;
gave her golden bangles first;
then gave the chain on her neck;
and finally the jewel studs.
Gandhi, moved and pleased,
concealed his wonder.
Asked if she sought her parents' consent.
Her father there nodded.
Kaumudi pledged to wear no ornament;
she led a simple humble life;
taught Hindi in Malabar schools;
closely followed Gandhi's footsteps;
taught national language
till her death at ninety two.
Kaumudi's dazzle dimmed
the dazzle of all other women in jewels and ornaments.
Let's bow our head to this rarest gem.

Vadakara, Malabar are places in the State of Kerala in India.

Questions
- Who was Kaumudi Teacher?

How I Became a Vegetarian

My mind used to taunt me:
"Hey Mister, incongruous
are your words and actions;
what do you write and teach?
The relation between
Man and Nature and God;
human beings and other beings,
all children of God;
Man has no right
to torture any other being.
Hey Mister, have you no shame
to eat the flesh of
innocent animals and fish?"
Born a Christian,
lived a non-veg life;
believed the teachings
that man is the centre of universe;
God made other beings
for his food and assistance.
Millions live in illusions.
Gandhi is my role model;
my eyes are opened at last
and I have become
a pure vegetarian.

Questions
- What made the poet a vegetarian?

Michael Jackson, King of Kings

Michael Jackson,
thou art gone;
beckoned back
to feast His senses.
Angels sing and dance
to your lightening steps.
You were the king of kings,
both of music and dance.
Reigned the world
for several decades;
risked your body,
and challenged the White.
Could win millions' hearts,
both White and Black;
staked your health
for the fulfilment of art.
Irreplaceable is the loss--
The chasm widens
in width and depth;
many who try or shall try
to bridge
will feel the folly.

Questions

- How did Michel Jackson stake his health for the fulfilment of art?

Synopsis

Winged Reason, a collection of poems by K. V. Dominic is about losses, including the ultimate loss which is the most unrelenting and grimmest loss of human life. It appears that the poet has experienced those losses himself or has heard closely the cries of the bearers of those losses. The first poem begins with a question, which is the quintessence of the *Winged Reason*. The question probes philosophers and touches the innermost chords of its readers.

The fount of the poet's inspiration is humanity that encourages readers to realize that the earth is the home for all and as members of the same family all should hear the heartbeat of others. The poet does not hesitate to attack wherever he finds injustice. His prime victims include hollow rituals, traditions, inequity, inhumanity, freedom and exploitation in every shape. The poet is a master in painting touching pathos of the pangs, whether of a widow, a kidnapped boy, Tsunami Camps, Indian democracy, or inane religious dogmas. Since the message is crucial to the poet, his style is straightforward and without imprecision in meaning and moral view.

The poet's artistic passion to help the helpless is obvious, particularly in "A Blissful Voyage" where he aspires to have wings to see the places where injustice reigns. In the next poem, "A Nightmare," he turns into a hawk to view the scene of absurdities. In "International Women's Day", the representative poem, he is absolutely appalled at the conditions under which women are treated. This and several other poems are not easy to read because they explore the evils and hurts of the soft targets of the country.

Reviews

Winged Reason, the first collection by K. V. Dominic, deserves to be read and evaluated closely and widely. I recommend that poetry lovers and libraries keep *Winged Reason* on their shelves because it enriches, no matter from which portal they enter the panorama of the valleys and hills of this volume.

--Dr. Stephen Gill, Indo-Canadian Poet, Canada, October 2009

K. V. Dominic, like Professor Shiv K. Kumar, is also a late bloomer in the world of Indian English poetry; but in this very first volume of poems he exhibits his penchant for social themes such as religious harmony, poverty, corruption, suffering, human cruelty, mafia crime, old age problem of aloofness, misappropriation of money, haves and have-nots, problems of the handicapped, female foeticide, the evil of dowry, disparity, unemployment and neglect of intellect in India. In addition to these themes, the poet has also taken care of dignity of labour, service unto God, maternity, beauty and also two elegies on death. There is no doubt that his contribution to Indian English poetry will definitely enrich and leave it more mature and richer for the posterity.

--Dr. D. C. Chambial,
Poet, Critic and Editor: Poetcrit, Maranda, HP, India.

Dr. K. V. Dominic, an English teacher of repute, and gifted with a great critical sensibility, is the Editor of the internationally-refereed *IJPCL*. His poetry stands out in simplicity, substance and style of his muse. What immediately strikes even a casual reader of his poems is his wide humanistic concerns in the all-happening life around; it may reflect his impatience and incoherence verging on incongruity also.

Dominic's sincerity of purpose and truthfulness of presentation add to the strength and beauty of his poetic artistry, fast shaping him to carve a respectable place among the greats of Indian English Poetry.

--Sudarshan Kcherry, Publisher, Authorspress/Gnosis

About the Author

K. V. DOMINIC (born 1956) Indian English poet, critic, editor and short story writer is a faculty member of the PG & Research Department of English, Newman College, Thodupuzha East P. O., Idukki District, Kerala, India, Pin: 685585. He was born on 13 February 1956 at Kalady, a holy place in Kerala where Adi Sankara, the philosopher who consolidated the doctrine of Advaita Vedanta was born. Prof. Dominic has been teaching UG and PG students since 1985. His research topics are "Pathos in the Short Stories of Rabindranath Tagore" and "East-West Conflicts in the Novels of R. K. Narayan with Special Reference to *The Vendor of Sweets, Waiting for the Mahatma, The Painter of Signs* and *The Guide.*" He is the author of the books, (1) *Postcolonial Readings in Indo-Anglian Literature,* (2) *Selected Short Stories in Contemporary Indo-Anglian Literature,* (3) *Pathos in the Short Stories of Rabindranath Tagore* and (4) *Reason and Fantasy* (Poems and Short Stories). International Poets Academy, Chennai has conferred on him the LIFETIME ACHIEVEMENT AWARD "in recognition of his distinguished contribution to World Poetry, and for his pioneering pursuits in influencing mankind towards the path of World Peace, Global Harmony and Cosmic Humanism." Prof. Dominic has written a number of poems, critical essays and short stories in reputed journals and books. As the Editor of *Indian Journal of Postcolonial Literatures (IJPCL),* a reputed international refereed biannual (ISSN 0974 – 7370) published by the Centre for English Studies, Newman College, Thodupuzha, Kerala, India, he is a well known figure in the universities, colleges and such academic circles all over India. He is in the Advisory and Editorial Boards of several leading journals in India.

Cover Illustrations by: K. K. Anas, Paris

Write Son, Write
K. V. DOMINIC

Dedicated to
My Beloved Mother,
(Late) Rosamma Varghese,
Kannappilly

Contents
Book 2 -- Write Son, Write

Preface	67
Foreword	69
Write My Son, Write	74
An Elegy on My Ma	89
Victory to thee, Mother India	92
Massacre of Cats	94
A Cow on the Lane	97
A Desperate Attempt	98
Attachment	100
Aung San Suu Kyi—Asia's Lady Mandela	102
Bravo Katie Sportz!	103
Coconut Palm	104
Crow, the Black Beauty	105
Flowers' Greetings	106
For the Glory of God	108
God is helpless	110
Hunger's Call	112
IAF Vayu Shakti 2010	113
Musings from an Infant's Face	115
Nature Weeps	117
Resolution	120
Rocketing Growth of India!	121
Sister Mercy	123
Teresa's Tears	124
To My Colleague*	126
Train Blast	128

Tribute of Mohammed Rafi 130

Wagamon 131

Water, Water, Everywhere 133

Wolfgang, the Messiah of Nature 135

To My Deceased Cats 136

Lines Composed from Thodupuzha River's Bridge......................... 138

Reviews 139

About the Author 140

Preface

This is my second collection of poems, an outcome of my fourteen months' poetic voyage from September 2009 to November 2010. My first anthology, *Winged Reason*, was the outpouring of my five years' itching mind. The long difference in the tenure shows that my mind has been becoming more and more unrest. Naturally, the more unjust and disquiet the world becomes, the more distressed and desperate would be the poet's mind.

As poetry is the shortest form of literature, most captivating and didactic, I believe that in this busy, hustling world people should have a special attraction to poetry. Since reading habits of modern man diminish considerably and she/he substitutes that habit to watching TV and such visual media, I believe that it is my duty as a writer to promote poetry at any cost. I have already published four edited books consisting of innumerable critical articles on the poetry of established and emerging contemporary Indian poets in English.

People today are crazy after materialism, and divinity in them is being lost to such an extent that they give no importance to principles, values, family and social relations, cohabitance with human beings and other beings. Instead they are trying their maximum to exploit their fellow beings, other beings and the planet itself. If it goes like this, the total destruction is not far away. It is the duty of the religious leaders, political leaders and the intelligentsia to inject the lost values to the masses and thus preserve this planet and the inhabitants from the imminent devastation. Instead, majority of these leaders become mafias and inject communal and corruptive venom to the minds of the masses. Corruption has become the hallmark of these leaders and influenced by them the masses also deviate from the right track to the evil track. And who will save this society? My answer is: writers, particularly poets who are like prophets.

Though the present century, like the previous one, is that of fiction, there are innumerable great poets and great poems in English literature as well as literatures of other languages. Fiction has become an addiction to the present readers. The publishers and the award committees are responsible for this addiction. They can very well change the tastes of the readers if they will. Let me emphasise and underline once again that there have been greater poems to the great fictions which have won the awards in this decade as well as in the previous ones. Save a few established Indian poets in English, majority of the Indian poets writing in English publish their excellent anthologies spending thousands from their pockets. Journals are their only haven where they can post their individual poems just taking the subscriptions. Indian poetry in English should be promoted by the governments, both central and states, by giving awards and grants to the poets because it is the mouthpiece through which India proclaims her great values, ethos, cultures, traditions, myths, legends, landscapes, faunas, climates etc. to her own children and people abroad. Schools, colleges and universities in India should include more of this poetry in the text books.

There are thirty poems in this anthology. The opening poem "Write Son, Write" is indeed the manifesto of my views and philosophy. Divided into twenty one parts, it declares my views of God, Man and Nature. There are two poems in this book which were born out of my tears. My mother, to whom I owe all my virtues, departed me on 14th October 2010. From the deep sorrow came out the poem "An Elegy on my Ma." This book itself is dedicated to her. A month later, my neighbour, a man of high rank in the society, poisoned to death all my four favourite cats which made our house a heaven. This massacre was as shocking as my ma's death and it gave birth to the poem "Massacre of Cats." Even now I am drowned to agony whenever my mind draws me to those tragedies.

Before winding up my preface let me express my deep gratitude to Mr. Sudarshan Kcherry, the publisher of Authorspress, New Delhi. He is a mentor to me in shaping my philosophy. I have put into the poems whatever philosophy I could absorb from him. I don't believe if there is any other publisher in the world who inspires his writers to their works and publish the books never worrying about the material gain. The contribution this man does to Indian literature in English, particularly poetry, is greater than that of the greatest English writer in India. Hats off to him, and let his breed multiply!

Finally I present a bouquet of thanks to Mr. K. K. Anas, the cartoonist and illustrator of this book. He is my former student who is doing PhD now in France. Anas is an acclaimed cartoonist who drew illustrations for my first anthology *Winged Reason* also. Thanking once again everyone who inspired me and helped me in the composition of this book and wishing my readers a mental feast, I wind up.

K. V. Dominic

Foreword

In *Write Son, Write* K. V. Dominic is truthful and gracious to artistic ingenuity like his earlier collection of poems *Winged Reason*. Here, the poet appears to carry forward and strengthen the argument of social reform he initiated in "Winged Reason." This provokes man to think deep. Contemporary times are a challenge to true art and creativity. An age of crisis at multiple levels with epileptic anarchy defies definition. A simple living is gravely imperilled by impatience and frustration particularly at the grassroots-stage. If life is observed intimately, the crisis appears forbidding. Dominic's social consciousness is his chief forte. Not for a moment, he diverts attention from the simple and innocent activities of ordinary human beings. From his lyrics originate feelings of eternal sympathy, peace and fraternal unity.

One discerns a distinct pattern in thoughts and feelings. Deep down, one finds a divine presence in each part of the body. One is stunned by an immensely touching verse, "An Elegy on my Ma." The lyric, if at one level, speaks of an intense personal tragedy; it also generalizes a man's attitude to relations and thus a callous truth is revealed. Its' delicate treatment stirs sensitive hearts, and delicately but brusquely speaks for all of us. How children worship and then ignore Ma. Perhaps, in oblique words, the poet laments at the heartlessness of children. A similar fate visits a man at the fag end of life but still one rarely learns to value relations, the poet appears to say. *"Write My Son, Write"* is a long engaging verse that celebrates creation's inherent blessings in living and non-living. Nature is not only a symbol of destruction but it is harmony and symphony incarnate with profusion of love. The poet wants vividly to acquaint the growing son about nature and the world of man. Nature is caring, divine and loving whereas man is violent, cruel, selfish and egoist. At another level, it is God's divine dictates to His children on earth to work in the spirit of prayer and it will lead man to meaning and fulfilment.

Man never quite easily works for peace and love. Religion and knowledge look empty. Political weapons and corporate culture humiliate creations of God and if one tries to unearth solutions with the power of intellect, an absolute hypocrisy drives man to imminent disaster, he appears to say. Rhythm in each particle, molecule and atom of this world is what, a man must understand and there exist peace, harmony and symphony of life. The poet is not irrelevant when he speaks painfully about the role of intellectuals and religious people while observing in "Write My Son, Write":

> Intellectual mafia
> assumes omniscient;
> exploits innocent people;
> detracts them
> . . . .
> imposes their
> obsolete philosophies.

He is sensitive and fairly poignant while observing the miserable living conditions of man and suggests that when man refuses to fall back on dead and archaic ideas, he can certainly touch borders of benign culture and civilized living because there is hardly any difference "between religious / and intellectual mafias." This long lyric reveals poet's philosophy of education. Poet's anxieties about human life and destiny are genuine when he experiences violent and inhuman, unsympathetic and callous attitude of man.

Man does not grow with puffed up ego and pride. By killing egoistic mind-set, life turns evocative. Poet's sympathies are reserved for women. He cannot withstand any harsh treatment meted out to women irrespective of age and status. A girl glues to the book in difficult times in an effort to realize aspirations of life when even nature in the shape of a cuckoo: "prays for her perseverance. / The gentle breeze strokes her / and soothes her tense mind." ("A Desperate Attempt") It provokes the poet to warn man of unkindly approach to life and indirectly the poet wants man to listen to nature and learn. As a firm humanitarian, he cannot hate God's creation and so love for the animal world is immense. He loves birds, insects and little flying objects. One gets a clear message - if man loves all, he will never hurt or impair not even beasts or snakes, for love knows no barriers.

The poet believes in the eternal principles of love, sympathy and non-violence. These are unifying forces and man lives harmoniously if he learns to love that is strengthened in the school of life. "Write my Son, Write" is one of the finest poems, for it is also a testament on life in gentle words. There is nothing intellectual or ethical or religious or political here. Man, if learns to live beyond hate and tyranny, violence and exploitation, possibly a better world would emerge. Even trivial acts or words do not escape poet's keen eyes and he eagerly scrutinizes low and high, small and big, the poor and the rich with impartiality. Abundant miseries and sufferings, in the life of the poor disturb. That, women still live in subjugation with fears and uncertainties, create upheavals in the mind of the poet. He condemns this attitude of male-dominated society. Poverty, hunger, corruption, sufferings, exploitation, inhuman outlook, waste of public money, subtle atrocities resorted to by the intellectual and political mafia cause agony to the poet. Uninterrupted and perpetual concerns about man's life on earth make Dominic's poetry unique. He is sensitive, eager and compassionate and is anguished at the all-consuming sufferings. Symbol of crow highlights venomous racial thinking proving lethal in the progress of man. Man may profess humanistic thoughts but the truth cannot be ignored that inherent battles among the white and black infect the world with hatred and violence when he says: "When will the Black and the White / dwell in the same house / ... When will we behold God's creation / with impartial eyes / and find His beauty in all forms." ("Crow, the Black Beauty") This sacred wish is the grace and nobility of a man with a humanitarian outlook. Poet is pained when he finds that the mother earth has been destroyed and contaminated. Nature is the worst sufferer. Man is injured within and disturbed outside. Though often reflects on fake contentment in life yet he is totally distraught and lives a mentally disjointed life. Even God feels vulnerable when the little kids pray. But nothing can be done to avert natural calamities.

The poet is obsessed with the thoughts of honesty, welfare and stately kindness. If he writes about hunger, it is a prayer to the rich. If he speaks about the sufferings of the poor, he also nurses a desire within where man should put an end to spending national wealth on items of destruction. Deeply hurt and ironical, he pleads to eliminate hunger and destitution with the weapons man creates to kill enemies. This is a mild outburst perhaps to strike an inert man. It is a call to the soul of man to awake to harsh truths, for, if sufferings visit man, none can be prosperous psychologically and materially. He is piercingly acerbic and hurts sensibilities when observes:

> Isn't poverty the greatest enemy?
> Why not fight against it
> and wipe out destitution,
> pointing guns, rifles and missiles
> at the chest of the poor?

("Hunger's Call")

These emotionally disturbing fulminations are genuine when he watches apathetic people. The poet understands the pretence so even if he condemns man's attitude in highly incisive tones, he suggests solutions to rampant poverty, hunger, greed and exploitation when he says: "God, kindle love / in the minds of all rulers. / Had they spent those billions / to feed millions' hungry mouths, / could save several millions / dying famished year after year." ("IAF Vayu Shakti 2010") Very rarely, creative artists display courage in terse and strident words. Look at the following lines:

> "... a horrible sight.
> The dropping of each missile,
> an explosion in my heart.
> My mind can't conciliate
>
> ("IAF Vayu Shakti 2010")

The poet's faith in God is amazing. He finds Him in each creation and if in the little kids he observes that "the creator is manifest in their faces" he speaks for all good souls reposing faith in God -a very quizzing and quibbling idea. His poetic characters are scattered around and the poet pays tributes to great souls, ordinary men and women who mitigate sufferings of mankind. In every living being he finds the spirit of God and if progress and growth are hinted at, he dislikes machine-like precision. Here, one is reminded of Aleksandr Solzhenitsyn's pertinent observations: "We must not simply lose ourselves in the mechanical flow of Progress, but strive to harness it in the interests of human spirit; not to become the mere playthings of Progress, but rather to seek or expand ways of directing its might towards the perpetration of good...we have lost the harmony with which we were created, the internal harmony between our spiritual and physical being." The poet appears to resurrect the meanings of these words.

He is profoundly influenced by Gandhi and Ruskin and believes that the true wealth of a society or nation is, man. If society works for the happiness of man, it creates real wealth. Implicitly, the poet makes it abundantly clear that sufferings born out of hunger and deprivations can be reduced if work is thought as a prayer and each one gets due shares. Like the great social scientists Gandhi and Ruskin, Dominic appears to maintain that many evils and distortions of modern civilization are contained not in the poverty and hunger but if everyone begins to take pleasure in the work and starts living life, it will make world, a better place to live. And here, he emphasizes the significance of altruistic Karma's theory of Gita.

There are very few poets who have shown so much anxiety and anguish towards the poor and the exploited. Dominic is a poet of the masses it is evident but he is not a philosopher. He wants social status with prestige to the poor and the miserable and thus he is a poet of the downtrodden. And so, these beautiful lyrics reveal that Dominic is an artist of social panorama. He lives where the heart of man is and that is poet's real strength.

P.C.K. Prem
(Retd. IAS Officer), English Poet, Critic, Fiction Writer
from Himachal Pradesh, India.

Write My Son, Write

Part One

My son,
I have a mission
in your creation,
God spoke
to my ears.
Why do you
look up?
Look at the tip
of your pen.
I am the ball
of your pen;
I am the ink
that flows
on the paper.
Write, my son,
write.
Write till
I say stop.

Part Two

Don't you feel
the symphony
of the universe?
It grieves me that
your species seldom
senses my rhythm.
Plants and animals
dance to my number.

Part Three

There is rhythm
and harmony
in every molecule;

every atom;
every movement;
the majestic tramp
of elephants;
dart of deer;
trot of tiger;
race of rabbit;
lope of leopard;
swoop of swine;
scud of squirrel;
canter of kangaroo;
tear of bear;
gallop of horse;
bound of bull;
dash of dog;
flutter of dove;
dart of cormorant;
plunge of kingfisher;
flit of swift;
flap of crow;
swoop of kite;
plummet of eagle;
wing of mynah;
buzz of bees;
drone of mosquito;
motion of snake;
march of millipede
and centipede;
and movements of
worms and insects.
Rhythm is there
everywhere
and creates
the perpetual
harmony.

Part Four

Write, my son,
write.
How rhythmic

is your body!
Rhythm is there
in your breath;
your heartbeats;
your eyewinks;
your walk and run;
your chew
and munch;
digestion in
your stomach;
your laughter
and your cry;
the words
you speak;
and even
your flatus.
Alas, you never
feel this wonder.

Part Five

Write, my son,
write.
Birds and animals play
their assonant keys.
Man alone strikes
discordant notes.
You do hear
the music of birds;
Hoot of owls;
coo of doves;
twitter of sparrows;
cackle of chicken;
cuckoo of cuckoo;
crow of raven;
squawk of parrot;
pipe of skylark;
chatter of magpie;
gobble of turkey;
song of nightingale;
chirp of swallow;

quack of duck;
and crow of cock.
Equally assonant,
the cry of animals.
Bark of dogs;
meow of cats;
bleat of sheep;
bray of donkeys;
roar of lions;
howl of fox;
hiss of snake;
and neigh of horse.

Part Six

Write, my son,
write.
Living beings and
lifeless objects
all inter-related.
Your existence
depends on others;
all my creations,
useful and beautiful.
It's your pettiness,
viewing things
in different ways,
thinking in opposites;
good and bad,
beautiful and ugly.
snakes, worms,
pests, mosquitoes,
ants, lice, beetles,
centipede, millipede,
cockroach, spider--
all for me, good
and beautiful;
but for you,
bad and ugly.
Your selfish mind
tries to ignore

benefits rendered
by these housemates.

Part Seven

Write, my son,
write.
Your species
can't live alone.
Cattle, sheep,
goats, donkeys,
dogs, cats,
swine, fowl,
I created
for your company;
neither can they
exist without you.
You speak to them
in strange tongue,
and they reply
in divine speech;
unintelligible,
you scourge and
even kill them.

Part Eight

Your species
is the latest
of my creations;
evolved after
millions of years
of progressive march.
progression
or regression?
Was my plan
wise or folly?
Doesn't it distress
and boomerang?

Part Nine

I risked a test
in man's brain.
Filled some cells
with seeds
of knowledge.
Alas! Vainglorious
he thinks
the master
of all wisdom;
tries to conquer
the universe:
landed on the moon,
sent satellite
to the Mars;
he takes it
greatest feat!
The Moon and Mars
just two drops
in the ocean of
celestial objects.
Poor creature
knows not
his handicap;
limitations of
his reason.

He defies me,
assumes my position,
haughtily claims
as the noblest
of my creations!
He gives me shape,
and boasts,
embodiment of God!

I breathed in him
celestial values:
happiness, beauty,
peace, love, mercy;

but he fosters
hate and violence;
kills his kith and kin;
shows no mercy
to animals and plants.

Part Ten

Christmas is your
greatest festival;
greeting each other
peace and happiness;
blackest day for
cattle, fowl and fish;
billions butchered
for your pleasure;
you dine and dance,
sing hymns of peace!
preach gospel of love!
Your happy celebrations:
birthday, marriage,
ordination, jubilee,
feasts and festivals,
doomsday for animals.
Their cries resound
like death knell
and thus you try
dissonance at
my harmony.

Who gave you right
to kill my creations?
The way you torture
fowl and cattle,
bereft food and water,
caged and chained,
gasp in sunlight;
you cut their throat
live to their eyes.
The fish you catch
struggle for breath

and cause your glee!

Part Eleven

Why don't you
learn from Nature?
Animals and birds
present you models.
Models of pure love,
happiness, hard work,
suffering, kindness,
patience, sharing,
fellowship, gratitude.

Part Twelve

Write, my son,
write.
Copy my symphony;
the music
of the universe.
Show your species
their deficiencies;
you can't catch
the musical charm
of gentle breeze;
the melody
of falling leaves
and petals;
the stroking music
of mist and snow;
divine language
of the insect world;
the hugging tone
of flies on flowers;

Part Thirteen

Write, my son
write.

You can't enjoy
the beauty
of lightning
and thunder;
your people think
thunder is my
sword of punishment.
Tell them son,
their celestial Father
never hates;
will never punish;
only showers love
and looks after
His creation.

Part Fourteen

Write, my son,
write.
I haven't given
you reason
to learn
all my plans.
I speak to you
and other beings
in diverse tones.
None else shudder
when I speak
through thunder.
The sound of air
produced in breeze,
gale, tempest,
all my diverse notes.
The sound of water
in brooks, rivers
seas, oceans,
also my own scales.
What you hear
is little;
much more lies
beyond your ears.

Part Fifteen

Write, my son,
write.
Your species
needs humility.
You are my own dear
as mosquito is.
The snake you fear;
the pests, insects,
rodents you hate;
virus, worms
and all you dread
are no less
dear to me
than you.
I speak to you
through cuckoo;
I lull you
through owl.

Part Sixteen

Write, my son,
write.
Teach your folk
their position.
All other beings aware
of their humble position;
only your species
ignorant of his position.
religious mafia,
political mafia,
intellectual mafia,
mislead
your innocent
humble folk.

Part Seventeen

Religious mafia
created thousands of gods.
Creator, creation, creature--
simple enough
to learn the relation.
Myriads of religions,
gods, saints, prophets;
religious mafia needs
them to exploit
innocent laymen.
Heaven and hell
they created
to frighten the masses.
Where is the heaven?
Where is the hell?
They have no answer;
they attribute
to their Creator
all their qualities:
Angry God!
Punishing God!
To appease me
they loot billions
from the laity!
Build palace-like
churches, mosques, temples;
decorate my fake images
with rich ornaments
and gaudy dress;
they misguide laymen;
make them believe
I am fond of flattery;
fond of hymns;
fond of money;
fond of food;
and fond of jewellery.
They never preach
Karma is the best prayer;
work is worship;

service to the poor;
service to the needy;
service to the tortured;
service to animals
and plants and trees
are services to me.
Look at the birds;
look at animals;
look at fishes;
look at plants;
they seek their food;
strike the eternal
note of happiness
and never digress
from the symphony.
The religious mafia
makes laymen blind;
blind in their faith;
they blind their reason;
poor folk, they dance
to their perfidious tones.

Part Eighteen

Write, my son,
write.
I have created man
herbivorous,
like his ancestors,
apes and monkeys.
The religious mafia
spreads its fake ism:
other beings and plants,
all for man's pleasures;
he is the king
of animals and plants.

The universe bears
sufficient food
for human and
non human beings.

all other beings
seek their food.
I haven't given
man licence
to kill other beings
as carnivores do.
Being the creator
I can't bear
the way man
rears, tortures
kills and eats
his domestic animals.

Part Nineteen

Write, my son,
write.
The political mafia
exploits masses;
dictates, strangles
and make them slaves;
imprisons, kills
those questions
their authority.
It's really shocking
your governments
plunder your people,
fill the exchequers
with trillions
to kill your own men
beyond the borders.
Political mafia
supports corporates,
ignores common folk,
sells land and resources
to inhumane companies.

Part Twenty

Intellectual mafia
assumes omniscient;
exploits innocent people;
detracts them
from their Creator;
makes them pessimists;
imposes their
obsolete philosophies.

No difference at all
between religious
and intellectual mafias;
twin sides
of the same coin.

Part Twenty One

Enough, my son,
enough;
nothing more
to tell your species.
If they heed
they will be saved;
other beings
will be saved;
plants will be saved
and the universe
as such will be saved.

Questions

- Why does God doubt if His plan of Man's creation was wise or folly?
- Why is Christmas the blackest day for animals?
- How do animals and birds present models to human beings?
- What are the deficiencies human beings have when compared to non human beings?
- Which are the diverse musical notes of God pointed out by the poet?
- Which are the mafias that mislead the people?
- How does religious mafia mislead and exploit the people?
- How does political mafia exploit the people?

An Elegy on My Ma

Ma, that smile on your face
ripples down
to a Tsunami of
grief in my mind.
The glow in your eyes
darts like lightening
to my burning heart.
Strange enough
my sorrow mounts
day after day
you descended
into the earth.
My mind dissents
your ultimate adieu.
Ma, I do remember
the brambly path
you treaded for decades:
How you raised
your brothers and sisters
when your parents died;
Struggled hard for sustenance
even after your marriage;
How much you suffered
bearing six sons
in your womb!
Ma, how can I forget
the way you reared us?
Dawn to dusk
worked on the farm;
Made the field fertile
with gallons of sweat.
We were never starved,
nor knew any poverty.
Ma, I am speared
with my haunting past.
How ungrateful
were your sons!
How disproportionate

was our love!
How can your cent percent
match with our ten percent?
Truly mother's love
is the purest love
and divine love.
Ma, your old age ailments
haunt me and torment me.
The "lassix" tabs which now
lie on your table,
for which you cried for
when you laboured for breath
well my sunken eyes.
Your sleepless nights,
sitting and wheezing,
when we were fast asleep,
and struggling thus for
long six years,
bewailing often
"Why doesn't God
call me back?"
and finally bed-ridden
for a long week
with no food
but a little water--
flashes through
my aching mind
to bleed it over
my streaming cheeks.
Ma, I couldn't be
at your bed-side
when you murmured
throughout night
"Call my children;
ask them sing."
Ma, had you
premonitions of death,
or had you dreams
of Death visiting you
with your coffin?"
for you were whispering

"Remove the box."
Ma, were you reluctant
to leave your children?
Ma, you were never
deserted by your children.
What would be our fate, Ma,
when we become old as you?
Who will care us
as we cared you
one after other?
"It's better not to
fret on morrow;
Surrender unto Him
who created you."
Ma, we will go ahead
boosted by your divine words.

Questions

- Explain the lines "How can your cent percent / match with our ten percent?"
- What are the divine words of Ma?

Victory to thee, Mother India

Victory to thee, Mother India;
for you did unite the races
divided on religion,
culture, language and colour.
A hundred years back
thy great son, Tagore
sang in praise of you.
Matha, you could rouse then
the hearts of Punjab, Sind, Gujarat,
Maratha, Dravida, Orissa and Bengal.
Your face has turned now sad and gloomy,
for thy children heed you not,
but surrender their souls to communal devils.
Patriotism, nationalism, secularism
give way to
terrorism, communalism, and regionalism.
Matha, thy name was echoed
in Vindhyas and Himalayas;
 birds, and breeze and leaves
chanted your name.
but no birds are there now;
neither trees nor pure air.
Yamuna, Ganges and the oceans
woke up then, cheered by your blessings.
Bearing now carcass, plastic, garbage,
and all such filthy human trash,
thy rivers and oceans face their death.
Matha, I know the cause of your tears:
Religious, political, intellectual mafias
tear thy heart and drink your blood.
Tagore, Gandhi and Nehru
were your great sons;
no doubt, your womb
will bear more great children,
who will lift us from this trance
and tether us back to the global home,
and you will sleep on the lap
fondled by your Mother World.

Questions
- Why has Mother India's face turned sad and gloomy now"
- What is the cause of Mother India's tears?

Massacre of Cats

My next door neighbours,
husband and wife,
pious to the core,
go every morning
to church for Mass:
offerings to God.
Went this morning,
offering delicious
fish fry to all our
cute cats:
fish fry mixed with
highly virulent toxin.
Offerings at home;
offerings at church.
One after other,
all the four died,
struggling hysterically
for water and breath,
soft velvety fur
drenched in saliva
and excrement.
Heartbreaking carcasses
welled our eyes
and tears ran
like rivers.
With shaking hands,
dug a deep grave
and buried them.
The neighbours
celebrated the offer
peeping through
the window curtain.
How could they do this
demonic massacre?
They had complained,
the cats excreted
on their vast compound.
Cats always conceal

their excrement
with soil around.
Man has to learn a lot
from these humble beasts.
Where will
cats defecate?
Where will
all animals defecate?
Is this planet
man's sole property?
My materialist neighbours
go to church everyday;
read the Bible everyday;
but never read the part
to love other beings
as fellow beings.
Instead they believe,
other beings are
creations for their
service and taste.
God, instil in them
thy creation's purpose;
the need to love
other creations--
animals, plants
and the planet itself.
Kindly teach them
to learning to live
with the system.
Let my neighbours expiate,
dig out skeletons
of my cats;
tie them
to their necks
as Coleridge's
ancient mariner
did a century back
since he killed
the ominous albatross.
God, open the eyes
of all human beings

and show them
the flow of the universe
and make them all
as participatory beings.

Questions
- What according to the poet are the Creation's purpose?
- Which poem of Coleridge is alluded by the poet in this poem?

A Cow on the Lane

The train will leave at 5 am;
fifteen minutes remain,
and five more miles to drive.
Lo, a cow lies on the lane;
the horn sounded stormily.
The cow retorted smiling:
"Don't disturb my slumber."
Her posture reminds me
of Hanuman blocking
the journey of Bhimasena,
seeking kalyanasaugandhika
flower for his Draupadi;
how elder brother Hanuman
pricked his arrogant brother's
bubble of ego and insolence.
"Dear cow, kindly clear the road,"
I pleaded her with folded hands.
"This world is not your grandpa's.
It's so vast and wide.
Can't you take another route?"
What she said is right.
Like Bhimasena, my ego crumbled;
I drove my car backwards;
took another lane and reached
the station just on time.

Questions
- What is the message of the poem?
- Which Indian epic is alluded by the poet in this poem?

A Desperate Attempt

Nothing under the sky
can distract Favitha;
no vehicle,
no pedestrian,
no commotion,
no photographer.
She is intently preparing
for tenth class exams.
A milestone is
her writing desk;
a boulder her stool;
a vaka tree gives her
shelter from scorching heat.
Nearby is her hut;
thatched single room cell;
living with her
parents and brother;
Illegal abode on roadside.
The vaka tree blesses her,
showering myriads
of yellow flowers.
The cuckoo in full throat,
prays for her perseverance.
The gentle breeze strokes her
and soothes her tense mind.
Favitha's dreams
and aspirations
have started to germinate.
Will it grow to a full tree,
giving shelter to her
parents' shattered life?
Won't her ambitions
be pricked by today's
capitalistic world order?

Questions
- What is the desperate attempt of Favitha?

- How is Favitha blessed by the Nature?

Attachment

Poppy, my dearest kitten;
God gave me through my friend.
Manifestation of Him in her face;
echoes my house with His sounds;
fills my heart with untold bliss.
Her serene sleep on my lap;
gentle bites on my fingers;
sharing of my own food;
football play to please me;
cause for me to immense glee.

My affection to Poppy
no less than to my wife,
daughter and son.
What difference is there
between men and animals?
For He resides in all.
Why should I seek Him
in churches and prayer halls?

I am much grieved by Poppy's loss;
left me by chance in a friend's car;
escaped from it on the way.
Is she living or dead?
Is she seeking still her mother
who has forgotten her presence?
Why is man so over-sentimental?
Why is he too much attached
to earthly and finite things?
God, teach me how to detach;
and also teach my neighbours
and millions of my brothers and sisters
to show love and mercy
to all non human beings

Questions
- What is the poet's prayer to God?

- Where does God reside, according to the poet?

Aung San Suu Kyi—Asia's Lady Mandela

This is my prayer to you, Mahavishnu:
will you descend to Myanmar
in any perfidious guise you choose;
as you descended in Kerala
when Maveli ruled there;
and envious of his golden rule,
stamped him to the underworld.
Here is your chance to expiate;
dispatch the tyrants and
release the dove from the cage.
Let Suu Kyi fly over Myanmar
shower rays of freedom;
break the locks of the cells,
and millions breathe
the vibrant air of liberty.
Suu Kyi, the epitome of valour,
showed her people through her life
liberty is born from the ashes of fear.
Her twenty years of political life;
more than fourteen in solitary cells.
Pledged to continue in Myanmar
till the last compatriot exists.
Suu Kyi is the super-magnet;
no cell can obstruct her power;
millions are drawn to her.
She will turn to be an atom bomb,
explode at the military headquarters
and save Myanmar from the dictators.

Questions

- Who is Aung San Suu Kyi?
- What are the objects Suu Kyi compared to?

Bravo Katie Sportz!

Katie Sportz, twenty two:
the youngest solo across the Atlantic.
The entire human race
bows its head before you.
You are the icon of women's valour;
a scud missile darting through patriarchy.

Long seventy days and nights,
with only sun, moon, stars as companions;
eating only freeze-dried meals and dried fruits;
risking hurricanes of twenty-foot waves;
reminding heroes of legends and fairy-tales;
rowed four thousand five hundred and thirty four
kilometres with no help from mainland.
Not only satiated thirst for adventure
but raised seventy thousand US dollars
for the project of Blue Planet Run Foundation,
supplying drinking water round the globe.
I bow my head before you;
Let your race fill this planet

Questions
- Who is Katie Sportz?
- Why does the poet compare her to a scud missile?

Coconut Palm

Tall and majestic coconut palm
shot like a rocket to the sky
with a brilliant view of
sparkling leaves and alluring nuts.
Best friend of human beings;
foot to tips not any inch useless.
Standing erect on lean tall foot
and growing up to hundred feet
bearing tones of leaves and fruits.
A marvel to all architects.
No human hand can build
such a parallel pillar.
Kudos to the Architect of architects!

Questions

- How is coconut tree a marvel to all architects?
- Why is coconut tree called the best friend of human beings?

Crow, the Black Beauty

Crow, the commonest bird in the world;
cleaner of kitchen garbage;
has seldom been sang
in praise by the poets.
The poets hail cuckoo, skylark, nightingale.
Parasite cuckoo lays her eggs
in compassionate crow's nest.
Unfortunate crow feeds cuckoo's chicks;
yet crow is not lauded
and cuckoo is extolled.
Crow's counterpart dove;
icon of love and innocence.
Why is white attractive
and black disgusting?

When will "crow-crow" be
pleasing as "koo-koo"?
When will the Black be
kindred to the White?
When will the Black and the White
dwell in the same house
and dine from the same plate?
When will we behold God's creation
with impartial eyes
and find His beauty in all forms?

Questions
- What is the message of the poem?
- What does crow symbolize?

Flowers' Greetings

As I opened
front door
of my house,
roses smiled at me
and greeted,
"Good Morning, Sir."
I smiled back,
locked the door
and got down the steps.
I noticed the petals
waving at me
"Bon Voyage!"
The lilies then
wished me,
"Good Health!"
Thanking them
I drove
to the University.
On my return
in the evening,
parked at a bakery
to buy some bread.
Noticed a flower shop
beside the bakery.
Roses and lilies again;
pale and dismal;
decorated on a wreath.
I looked intently;
they weren't smiling;
heard them murmur,
"Happy Death!"
I was stunned.
Time for me
to leave the world?
No, they wish thus
to all onlookers,
I consoled myself.

Questions
- Why do the flowers murmur "Happy Death"?
- What contrast do you find in this poem?

For the Glory of God

(Based on *The Malayala Manorama Sunday Supplement* Report on 25th July 2010)

Chellamma Antharjanam, aged seventy five;
widow, childless, weak and homeless.
Rejected by relatives, neighbours and society,
decides to end her life on a railway track.
Counting down minutes, she timorously waits;
the alien Death will arrive in train
and take her to a happy abode.
Then Resiya Beevi, member of Panchayat,
drags her out from the claws of Death.
Risking taunts from kith and kin
takes her home to support her.
Resiya lives with her spouse and four kids.
Takes her guest as her own dead ma.
Service unto her, service to Allah.
Chellamma being a vegetarian Brahmin,
Resiya takes her to an old-age home;
bears all expense for her happy residence.
Meeting Chellamma's wish
to live her end in her own soil,
Resiya buys a plot
and builds a small house,
awaiting government's grant.
Resiya spends for the food
which Chellamma cooks and eats.
Ten long years have passed
since heaven thus exhibits here.
An exquisite model of
communal harmony!
Resiya's life is an ideal Muslim's life;
all will agree that God is pleased.
Resiya's own State witnessed another act:
religious extremists hacked off
a professor's right palm
and cut his legs to slaughter him.*

And they did this to please their God!

* The unfortunate incident took place on 4 July 2010.

Questions
- Why did Chellamma Antharjanam want to end her life?
- Why is called Resiya's life an ideal Muslim's life?

God is Helpless

The congregation wailed
after their parish priest:
"God, save us
from this extreme heat;
save us from the drought;
Merciful and Almighty God,
grant us rain,
and save our land."
Suddenly heard
a sound from above:
"I am helpless,
my beloved children.
I did supply
whatever you needed;
The same I gave
to all non-human beings;
I created the earth,
an oasis for men,
animals and plants;
unlike others,
you are selfish to the core;
despite your reason,
you are a nincompoop;
who will axe
the branch he sits?
How will you survive
without plants and trees?
You get rains
since trees are there;
where are the forests
which blocked the clouds?
The sun is the same;
its heat is the same.
Who told you to emit
toxic gas and defile
the sky, pure and clear?
Your wells are dry,
Rivers are dry;

I am not responsible.
You have dug your grave,
And what am I to do?
Petitions come to me
one after another
from plants and animals.
All complain of
your cruelty and torture:
they have no food;
they have no water;
they have no shelter;
and not even air.
They plead me
to call you back;
save their lives,
and thus save the planet.
Kindly tell me, children,
what shall I do."

Questions

- Why did God tell the congregation that He is helpless?
- What are animals' and plants' petitions against man?

Hunger's Call

A startling news with
photos from Zimbabwe!
Carcass of a wild elephant
consumed in ninety minutes!
Not by countless vultures
but by avid, famished
men and women and children.
Even the skeleton was axed
to support sinking life with soup.
Impact of globalization,
liberalization and privatization?
Or effect of hyperinflation
and economic mismanagement?
Billions are spent
by developed nations
on arms and ammunitions.
Isn't poverty the greatest enemy?
Why not fight against it
and wipe out destitution,
pointing guns, rifles and missiles
at the chest of the poor?

Questions

- What is the impact of globalization, liberalization and privatization?
- What does the poet sarcastically suggest to the developed nations to wipe out destitution?

IAF Vayu Shakti 2010

Indian Air Force
demonstrates Fire Power
at the desert of Pokhran:
"Vayu Shakti 2010."
President, Defence Minister,
officers, VIPs fix
their eyes at the sky.
Proud moments for them
and for several millions
sitting before the TVs.

But for me a horrible sight.
The dropping of each missile,
an explosion in my heart.
My mind can't conciliate
though only a parade.
These aircrafts have been built;
these missiles have been made
not for just a display.
One day or other
my sisters and brothers
in Pakistan and China
will be burnt with such missiles.

Major share of nation's budget,
much more than spent on food,
amassing arms, ammunitions, missiles.
Billions have been spent
by my country and
my neighbouring countries
and all developed countries
to kill their fellowmen abroad:
upright men and women and children.
Who are major victims of war?
Civilians as innocent as lambs;
ignorant of the bogus rift
between border nations.
Even the warriors who die:

Die martyrs for their motherland;
have no rancour for their opponents;
they are all puppets
in the hands of vile rulers.

God, kindle love
in the minds of all rulers.
Had they spent those billions
to feed millions' hungry mouths,
could save several millions
dying famished year after year.

Vayu Shakti: aeronautical power

Questions
- What political criticism do you find in this poem?
- Who are major victims of war?

Musings from an Infant's Face

(Composed on 8 March 2010—International Women's Day)

An infant over
her mother's shoulder
looked at me
from the front seat
of the bus I travelled.
Infants always
tempted me
like bloomed roses.
Babies—human
and non-human—
are embodiments
of grace and innocence.
The Creator is
manifest in their faces.
Blake's poems
of Innocence
and Experience
flashed through my mind.
I tried to smile
at the infant;
she didn't smile back.
Might be my
smile is guile and vile.
Her eyes seemed
to tell me something.
Her mother's appearance
foretold the infant's lot.
Born to poor parents,
how thorny would be
the path of her life!
She is yet to toddle;
I could vision
the blood oozing from
her soft feet.
Being a female,

black and dark,
poor and low caste,
discriminations,
humiliations,
abuses and tortures,
will come in battalions
to give her
Guard of Honour
and lead her along
the brambly path.
Lame and tottering
she will struggle along
till she reaches
her terminus, death.

Questions
- What wounding thoughts does the infant's face create in the poet's mind?
- Who will give Guard of Honour to the infant when she grows old?

Nature Weeps

Mango leaves droop:
irrational man ill-treated
gods of summer showers

Paddy fields lament:
none to reap ripened corns
sprouted and heavier

Lilly flower looks
reddish and morose:
had a shower in acid rain

Baby's incessant cry
makes her ma moan:
mercury reads forty two

People got out of their
houses at midnight:
electricity failed

Tigers started roaming
seeking food in villages:
people killed their preys

Crows and mynahs
stopped visiting me:
papaya trees bear no fruits

The sun is angry
and merciless to man:
man goes on felling trees

The child is reluctant
to go to school:
teacher welcomes with cane

Lotus bud weeps:
Fumed, cloudy firmament
hides the sun from kissing

Morning sun gloomy:
scattered dead bodies
killed in bomb blast

Cuckoo sings at midnight:
festival lights and fireworks
tumble cuckoo's slumber

Roses aren't smiling:
stinky insecticides
keeps flies from embrace

Spring's birth very late:
winter's blanket
turned up ice sheet

Mellow mango
clings to branch:
man will destroy its nut

Cow cries continuously
since calf doesn't suck:
artificial cattle feed

Cuckoos sound changes:
inhaled plastic fumes
spread in the sky

Gandhi's statue smiles:
could serve as seats for birds
longing for a birch

Cuckoos don't wake
me up in morning:
they have no trees to sit

Rainbows appear
only on papers:
no moist in the sky

Snakes appear on
roads and lanes:
their havens are furnaces

Mice and rats multiply
and trouble human beings:
man litters food around

Mosquitoes accompany
man day and night:
man breeds them unawares

Parents are very sad,
for little daughter has period:
hormonic chicken daily food

The boy goes to school
stooped and exhausted:
ten kilo books on his back

Questions
- Why do cuckoos sing at midnight?
- Why does Gandhi's statue smile?

Resolution

I couldn't believe my eyes;
neither the pedestrians gathered.
All eyes were fixed on the sky.
A woman on a tall thorny tree;
sharp spines covering
trunk, branches and twigs.
Standing on a bamboo ladder,
a score feet high,
shaming men she's
felling thorny branches;
support trees for pepper cuttings.
When few men risk
such hazardous labour,
necessity goaded her
to fight against fate.
Bed-ridden father and mother;
husband eloped with a harlot,
leaving her three daughters,
ten and twelve and fourteen.
She can earn more money
without such risk or pain.
Dignity and self respect--
she takes as greatest wealth.
Her resolution reminds me
of Wordsworth's Leech Gatherer
and Hemingway's Santiago.

Questions

- Why is the woman compared to Wordsworth's Leech Gatherer and Hemingway's Santiago?

Rocketing Growth of India!

Rocketing growth of India!
Overtaking America,
surpassing Europe,
competing with China.
The tornado of recession,
evolved in America
swept over Europe,
dashed towards Indian continent,
but drowned in the Indian Ocean.
Boasting and celebration
from government and ruling front!
Eyewashing by all media!
Statistics never fails.
First in population growth;
first in number of poor;
top in ignorance and illiteracy;
top in superstitions and fundamentalism;
very low standard of living.
Rocketing growth of the rich;
express growth of the poor;
multifold growth of their gap.
Slumdog Milllionaire is criticized:
exposed real growth of India.
Another tragic proof last day;
disproved country's bogus growth.
Thousand swarmed at ashram;*
poverty induced them to rush there
for a free square meal and
a present worth ten rupees.
Surging crowd collapsed
entrance gate to ashram.
Sixty three women and children
died in thousands' stampede;
many were injured and hospitalized.
Shocking news, details and photos
covered front page of newspapers.
PM announced ex gratia
of two lakhs each for the dead;

fifty thousand each for the injured.
Had the government granted
half the amount when they were alive;
had the government shown half the love
they shower to the rich,
many such tragedies be averted.
Still government and leaders
beguile innocent millions:
rocketing growth of our country,
a wonder to the whole world!

* Reference to the tragedy at Mangarh in Uttar Pradesh, India on 4 March 2010.

Questions
- What is the irony of the rocketing growth of India?

Sister Mercy

Sister Mercy, alias Daya Bhai;
a life worth her name.
Enticed into nunnery;
God whispered to her ears:
"Daughter, service to the poor
is superior to
prayers and hymns."
Risking rebukes and abuses
from parents, kith and kin,
quitted the four walls.

Devoted life for the tribal;
A lone-fighter for their right;
fought against slavery;
fought against girls' trade.
Hunted by the police;
torture in barracks;
Took LLB for self pleading.

Awards and honours
embraced her.
Even in her late sixties
this brave woman from Kerala
shines like the sun;
illumines thousands in Bykal,
A village in Madhya Pradesh.
Daya Bhai shows by life
that path of Karma is
nobler than other paths;
serving God in human form
is more rewarding than
serving Him in abstract terms.

Questions
- Who is Sister Mercy?
- What message does Sister Mercy give to the world?

Teresa's Tears

Teresa in tears
counting
thousands of rupees.
Part-time sweeper,
sweeping class rooms,
verandas, campus;
cleaning
dirty bathrooms,
stinky urinals.
First salary
after twelve months;
lump sum arrear
 thirty thousand.
Bed-ridden husband,
paralysed by accident;
two little daughters
in primary school;
life in a rented hut;
debts to neighbours.
Delicious food,
attractive dress,
only in dreams.
Counting currency
again and again;
tears running
like a brook.
"Teresa, why crying?"
Compassionate
headmaster
enquired her.
"Oh, nothing sir,
these are the notes
my hands worked for
and longed for;
but I have to keep
my promise;
a condition laid on
by the manager;

I have to donate
one year salary."
Government
gives the salary
but the building
not its property;
property
of the people.
Such forced donation
a canker of Kerala.

Questions
- Why is Teresa in tears?
- What canker of Kerala is depicted here?

To My Colleague*

(Composed on 15 August 2010)

India's sixty fourth Independence Day.
Celebrations all over the country.
Dear TJ, you are still dependent;
bed-ridden for forty three days.
Hacked-off right palm stitched to
like a dry branch budded to a live plant.
They axed your left leg from thigh to toes;
cut three fingers and bones of left palm.
Palms and foot in thick plaster.
Physical pains playing like concert;
added by arrows darted from all sides:
colleagues, university, government.
Helpless and sleepless, shedding tears often;
boldly bore pains of battalions
with convictions strong and unyielding will.
You prayed to God
to clear others' misunderstandings;
pardoned the assailants
who knew not
for what they had done it.
God heeded to your prayers;
removed all misunderstandings
from the minds of the millions.
They started showering
petals of love, sympathy and help.
TJ, you are a scapegoat;
people take you as a martyr.

India, my independent country!
Largest democracy in the world!
Largest secular State!
Equality, fraternity, liberty.
Liberty to do anything?
Where is freedom of speech
and expression?

India, my motherland.
Land of corruption, terrorism
and religious fundamentalism.
Religious fanatics resort to violence;
kill innocent masses
to appease gods in heaven.

TJ, you have become an icon;
an icon of suffering;
an icon of courage;
an icon of convictions,
and icon of forgiveness.

* The reference is to Prof. T. J. Joseph of Newman College, Thodupuzha, Kerala, India. Religious fanatics hacked off his right palm and threw it away when he was returning home after Sunday Mass on 4 July 2010.

Questions
- What is the theme of the poem?

Train Blast

Train blasted;
A hundred and fifty died;
All innocents;
Set out for
nearby destinations;
Ended at
eternal terminus.
Another heinous act
of Maoists.
End justifies means;
Misquote Marx
Lenin, Mao.
Utopian ends;
Diabolic means.
Are their hearts
made of stone?
Have their tears
dried in the furnace
of spite?
Have they plugged
their ears
with their
victims bones?
Heart-rending
is the wail
of that grandma:
"Krishna,
Why did you
call back
all my children?
What have they done?
Or their wives
and their children?
Couldn't you take
me also with them?
Krishna,
why are you
so indifferent?

Can't you punish
these terrorists
as you punished
Asuras?
Or at least
curse them
as you cursed
Ashwatthama?
How can I ease in
sambhavami yuge yuge?"

Questions

- Who is Ashwatthama?
- What is the cause of train blast?
- Bring out the irony of the lines "Ended at / eternal terminus."

Tribute of Mohammed Rafi

Mohammed Rafi flew back to heaven
thirty years back. Gandharva of music,
he was sent by God
to ease and solace burning minds.
Greatest of all Indian singers,
he was modest, dignified and humble.
Blessed by goddess Saraswathi,
he practiced hard for perfection.
When he raised his voice
to the highest octave,
to sing "O duniya ke rekhwale,"
blood oozed out of his vocal cord.
He walks with me in morning walks,
amusing me from cell phone.
His duets with Lata Mangeshkar,
his melodies that raise us to heaven,
impel me to call him:
"Immortality, thy name is Rafi."

Questions

- Who is Mohammed Rafi?

Wagamon

Wagamon,
Kerala's beautiful bonnet;
a spectrum of
spectacular scenes
carved all around it.

Steepish street
runs like anaconda;
sky-high precipice
on the right side;
hell-down caves
on the other side.
Miles long canvas
black and high;
green patches
here and there:
God with His brush!

A series of cataracts;
thin, thick, tall, short;
some like white paint
oozed from His brush;
others like curtains
slowly falling.
Eternal curtains,
eternal falling;
reminding us
the curtain of life.

Mounds after mounds;
green spongy eggs
placed in His large tray;
dawn to dusk
kissed by the sun;
the moon and the stars
embrace at night;
descending clouds
cleanse the dirt

treaded by humans.
Lying helpless
people speak to Him;
pray to Him
to ease their minds;
none will doubt here
the therapeutic
power of Nature.

Pine valleys of Wagamon,
an exotic wild beauty.
Tall and thick pine trees
support firmament
from falling.
God has spread
a fantastic carpet
knitted by
dry pine leaves;
lying relaxed,
people draft requests,
and angles descend
through the pine trees
and take these requests
to His office.
The sun is always gentle;
always seems an evening;
nocturnal music
of crickets,
resounding hymns of angels,
and semi darkness
lift our minds
to an eternal
abode of repose.

Questions

- What are the beauties of Wagamon?
- Bring out the imageries of pine valley.

Water, Water, Everywhere . . .

(Composed on 22 March 2000—World Water Day)

This day:
World Water Day;
tosses my mind
to the next century.
Water, the source of life;
Omnipresent and abundant
like its parent oxygen.
Free and 'insignificant'
for millions;
going to be more precious
than gold and diamond.

Absence of rains and trees,
enhanced by global warming,
exterminated millions of lives.
Life span dropped to thirty five;
thirty five looked eight five.
Dehydration caused wrinkles;
smooth skin turned
sore and scaly;
lovely long haired women
appeared shaved-headed ghosts.

Desalinated water,
the elixir of life.
In place of shower,
sponging with mineral oil.
Disposable dress;
heaps of garbage everywhere.

Water rationed;
per day quota
half a glass.
Kidney failure,
major cause of mortality.

Water stolen
at gun point;
armed forces guarded
water reservoirs of nations.

Sea level rose every day;
low lands disappeared
one after another.
Enactment of
Coleridge's lines:
"Water, water everywhere
Not a drop to drink."

Questions

- What are the dangers awaiting the world in the next century?
- Can you suggest a solution to avert the future danger?

Wolfgang, the Messiah of Nature

Wolfgang, the messiah of Nature
heard the silent call
of plants and animals;
flew from Berlin to Kerala
at the tender age of twenty.
Long forty years
in the midst of dense forest;
forest vast as fifty five acres;
Wolfgang's gift to man and Nature;
Swami to the neighbouring people;
God to plants and animals.
Twenty species of snakes,
fifteen types of amphibians,
two twenty species of birds,
sixty varieties of butterflies,
two thousand kinds of plants.
He has created a heaven;
a haven for his fellow creatures.
Snakes never bite him;
play with his children.
Birds never fear him;
always feast to his eyes and ears.
Butterflies weave him dreams;
a blissful dream which
blocks others' realities.
He has realized the truth,
the truth of eternal relations:
between God, Man and Nature.
Wolfgang is Nature's Christ;
born to redeem Nature;
his life is a sacrifice;
atonement for human cruelty;
expiation for felling and killing

Questions
- Who is Wolfgang?
- Why is he called the messiah of Nature?

To My Deceased Cats

"Lo, our Rocky is struggling;
God, is he departing us?"
Pussy cat cried to her friends.
"Has cruel man poisoned him?"
Pretty raised her doubts.
"Friends, my master, Mathew
mixed toxin to my dinner
since I excreted on his front yard,"
Rocky groaned while gasping.
"What a devil!" they exclaimed.
"Friends, I deserve this death.
I was a human in my last birth,
who hated cats and dogs.
I had a neighbour,
a poet and professor
who lived with his family
and half a dozen cats.
The cats knew no boundaries
and they often defecated
on my vast compound.
One morning before going to church
arranged for them delicious breakfast:
fried fish mixed with toxin.
I felt restless at church;
Christ on the cross
murmured to my mind:
'Is this the way
you love your neighbour?
Aren't cats and all other beings
your own neighbours?
Aren't animals and plants
our Father's creations?
Haven't they the right to survive?
Vowed to save lives
how can you destroy life?'
I tried my best to detract my mind;
turned my face from the crucifix;
calculated the profits

amassed from the rubber estates!
The Mass being over,
I returned to my house;
found my neighbour
digging graves for his pet cats.
The professor might have cursed me,
for he loved them as his children.
My happy life continued
as I was immensely rich.
Nothing happened to me,
But I couldn't rid His punishment;
and was reborn as a cat
to be killed by my own master."
Rocky ended with a loud wail;
his body shuddered and died.

Questions
- What is the message of the poem?
- Who was Rocky cat in his previous birth?

Lines Composed from Thodupuzha River's Bridge

Looking down from your girdle bridge
my eyes and mind bathe in thy morning beauty.
Invigorating cool water gushing through your vein
overflows my mind with eternal realities.
Every second passed in our lives
is irredeemably lost forever.
Invisible Time flashes in meteoric speed;
the waters I gaze now also flow beyond my eyes.
Unlike the flash of bygone Time
it is never lost but remains immortal.
Born from the eternal Sahyas
it merges into the eternal ocean.
The Creator thus reveals To His creations
His perpetual relation and incessant love.
Rivers and oceans are embodiments of cosmic reality.

Questions

- What is the philosophy the poet brings out through the river?

Reviews

"K. V. Dominic is a poet of quest. He seeks God's grace through service to humankind as he is aware of human beings themselves responsible for their plight. As he explores nature and environment, or exposes social degradation, or reflects on contemporary issues, he seems to justify the ways of God to man. He sounds critical of people who are self-centred and cause disharmony with their negative stances, be these related to scientific advancement, globalization, or pursuit of religion. With his strong personal beliefs and ideological commitment, Dominic seeks to resurrect the society, and effectively uses wit and irony. He also displays a sort of detached attachment as he reflects on war, poverty, deforestation, pollution etc, drawing on his rich regional experiences and poetic resources."

--Prof. R. K. Singh, Poet, Professor &
Head, Dept of Humanities & Social Sciences,
Indian School of Mines, Dhanbad, Jharkhand, India

This is the second volume of K.V. Dominic's poetry after *Winged Reason*, published in quick succession. Almost all his poems tell us that he never writes a poem to express sheer beauty, passion for possession, spiritual aspiration or aesthetic pleasure. He is a realist with deep social feelings. Human sufferings make his heart bleed, loss of freedom suffocates him. Not only human but animal sufferings too pain him. At some rare moments the nature lover in him appreciates nature's beauty or peeps into a cuckoo's nest. It is sad that though his imaginary creator created man ideally, he "fosters hate and violence." The well wishing poet prays, "Let Suu Kyi fly over Myanmar / shower rays of freedom."

--Aju Mukhopadhyay, poet, critic, short story writer,
essayist from Pondicherry, India

About the Author

Dr. K. V. DOMINIC (b. 1956), English poet, critic, editor and short story writer is a retired professor of the PG & Research Department of English, Newman College, Thodupuzha, Kerala, India - 685585. He was born on 13 February 1956 at Kalady, a holy place in Kerala where Adi Sankara, the philosopher who consolidated the doctrine of Advaita Vedanta was born. He has already authored and published nine books. Four other books of his are under print. Prof. Dominic has published innumerable poems, critical essays, reviews, interviews and short stories in reputed journals and books. He is the Secretary of Guild of Indian English Writers, Editors and Critics (GIEWEC), Chief Editor of the biannual, *International Journal on Multicultural Literature (IJML)* and editor of the Guild's biannual journal, *Writers Editors Critics (WEC)*. Dr. Dominic is also the editor of *New Fiction Journal (NFJ)*, an international annual on short stories. He is the Vice Chairman of International Congress for Language, Literature & Culture (ICLLC) and Vice President of IAPEN, Begusarai, India. He is in the Advisory and Editorial Boards of several leading journals in India. He can be contacted at:

prof.kvdominic@gmail.com
Land Phone: 04862 225758
Cell Phone: 9947949159
Web Site: www.giewec.com

Multicultural Symphony

K. V. DOMINIC

Dedicated to
My Bosom Friend and Chief Motivator
Sudarshan Kcherry

Contents
Book 3 -- Multicultural Symphony

Preface 145

Multicultural Harmony 149

Siachen Tragedy* 156

Horoscope 157

Global Warming's Real Culprits 158

Cohabitance on the Planet 159

Multicultural Kerala 161

On Conservation 163

Charles Darwin, Patron Saint of Animals 164

Elephant Mania 165

India, Number One! 166

Child Labour* 167

Caste Lunatics 169

Bulbuls' Nest 170

Beena's Shattered Dreams* 172

Mullaperiyar Dam* 174

I Wish I could Fly Back 176

Pearl's Harbour* 177

Dignity of Labour 179

Drowned Dreams* 180

Hungry Mouths 181

Ananthu and the Wretched Kite* 183

A Spider in My Bathroom 184

Fruit of Labour 185

Sail of Life 187

Valueless Education 188

Musings on My Shoes 190

Multilingual Black Drongo 191

Mukesh's Destiny* 192

Lottery Tickets Sellers 193

Mahi's Fourth Birthday* 194

Who am I? 196

Bathroom Monologues 197

Martyrs at the Borders 198

Mother's Love 199

Tears of a World Champion* 200

Thodupuzha Municipal Park 202

Why is Fate So Cruel to the Poor?* 204

Women's Cricket World Cup 2013 205

ACTS--Saviors on the Roads* 206

Beach Beauticians* 207

A Tribute to Sakuntala Devi* 208

Celebration of Girl-Child's Birth* 209

Where shall I Flee from This Fretful Land? 210

Homage to Swami Vivekananda* 211

Agitation through Farming* 212

An Ideal Festival* 213

Protest against Sand Mafia* 214

Synopsis 215

Preface

Multicultural Symphony is my third collection of poems after *Winged Reason*, published in 2010 and *Write Son, Write*, published in 2011. The only specialty of this collection is that the poems were composed after my retirement as Associate Professor of English. There is not much change in my themes or the poetic style.

Poetry is the best and easiest medium of imparting messages and values to the people. In this busy cyber age which is fast deteriorating in eternal human values, poetry has a great role in moulding cultured and civilized society, but the tragic irony is that none listens to the poets nowadays. Very few people cultivate reading habits and even if one reads something outside newspapers and periodicals they are fictions which entertain their minds. I don't think if any reader searches for a novel which conveys great messages or values. Poetry is the earliest form of literature and poets were considered seers everywhere. The tastes of the people have changed and they don't want to indulge in grave, philosophical or metaphysical thoughts. The evil influence of visual media and internet dissuades people from serious thinking. The tragic fate of poetry is universal and the poets are ignored worldwide. Literary awards most often go to fiction writers and there is no encouragement for the poets from any quarter.

Publishers are unwilling to take poetry as readers are few. Governments, academies, universities and other literary bodies do not promote poets by giving grants or incentives. I must specially congratulate my publisher Mr. Sudarshan Kcherry who has published maximum number of poetry books in India. It is because of his high ethical sense that he takes poetry collections one after another in spite of the huge loss of money from his pocket. He is indeed the poet of the poets and the critic of the critics. I can't find a comparison to him in the publishing world, at least in India. He is so unique that he inspires the writers with his intuition and the poetry flows from their pen unawares. My association with him is so deep that I am dedicating this book to him, who is my bosom friend and chief motivator.

Now coming to my themes in this book. Basically I am a follower of Advaita philosophy. Though I am a Christian by birth I believe in Adviata. My commonsense doesn't allow me to see God as a separate entity. I believe that that there is a Supreme Power or Energy which is controlling this universe. We call it God or the Creator. That power is the spirit or soul of the universe and its element is present in all its creations including atoms. Thus divinity is there in all bodies, both living and non living. Based on this reason I cannot find human beings better than other beings or dearest to the Creator as some religion teaches. Since the Creator has given reasoning power to human beings, they boast that the Creator is their own, having their own shape, and they only have souls which other beings lack, and other beings are inferior and are created for human beings' welfare and food etc. To me this universe is a big concert or symphony, a harmony of diverse notes. All creations play their role in concordance, but man tries to play discordant notes--stands against the rhythmic flow of the system. The inter-relationship between Man, God and Universe is the main theme of my poems. To me science and religion are two sides of the same coin. As man is the latest evolutionary being, he should respect other beings and plants which have greater legacy to claim in this universe. The intellectual capacity of man is used more for destruction than construction, more for vices than virtues. It is an irony that the more one is intellectual and educated the more he is vicious and crooked. Illiterate, rural people are more innocent and graceful than educated urban people. The leaders of the society--political, religious and intellectual—who should be models to the society, are very often worse than the rank and file or laity. They tend to act like mafia. This exploitation of the leaders, looting and torturing of the innocent masses, itch me almost every day and it gives birth to poems one after another. The huge devastation done to the nature and environment by sand mafia, forest mafia and quarry mafia goads me to react through my only medium, poetry. The fast widening gap between the poor and the rich--the vast majority deprived of food and shelter, indirectly caused by the greed of the two or three percent rich, bleeds my heart and results in several poems. Sexism or discrimination shown to woman as part of patriarchy is another wounding thorn which forces me to react through poetry.

Multicultural beauty of the universe, developed and developing nations' irrational craze for war and defence, sacrifice of soldiers for the nation, the need for peace relations between nations, superstitions created by religions and the exploitation of the laity by clergymen, global warming, need for conservation of nature, torture to elephants, child labour, casteism, unemployment, exploitation at the labour sector, dignity of labour, need of value based education, Swami Vivekananda's contributions, celebration of man's intelligence, skills and selfless service for society are other themes I have dealt in my poems. Sources for my themes are very often newspaper reports. I love to write more on concrete ideas than abstract ones.

I have only one motive behind my compositions—imparting some messages and values to the young minds which are groping in darkness and ignorance. Today's youth are disillusioned and they lead a futile life. They have no role models or messiahs to lead them in the right track. The clergy who are supposed to guide them are misleading them very often to fanaticism and religious fundamentalism. The same is the case with political leaders who never impart democratic, secular and patriotic values but partisan and parochial values to the young minds. Since the content of the poem is most important to me I don't mind if the lines lack the lustre of style. There are forty seven poems in this collection. I am presenting them before my esteemed readers who are the best judges to assess their quality. Once again thanking my dearest publisher, Mr. Sudarshan Kcherry for taking my humble work, I wind up my words.

K. V. Dominic

Multicultural Harmony

Part One

My dear fellow beings
when will you learn
the need for
multicultural existence?

The entire system
is a grand concert
composed by the Solespirit
As matter and spirit
animate and inanimate
visible and invisible
tangible and intangible
audible and inaudible
movable and immovable
are instruments multitudinous
of His perfect symphony.

Multiplicity and diversity
essence of universe
From atom to the heavens
multiculturalism reigns
This unity in diversity
makes beauty of universe.

What thrill is there in Sahara?
How dull is life in Atlantic?
Enchanting beauties of
gardens, groves, meadows,
fields, forests, woods,
brooks, rivers, cataracts
embodiments of multiplicity.

Multicultural instincts
exist in all creations
Inanimate beings know

how to flow with the system
Plant world too is
well aware of the system
Look at the woods
Look at the wild
Look at the birds
Look at the fish
Multicultural beauty everywhere.

It's we human beings who
distinguish and disintegrate
integrated animal world
Indian cow, American cow
African elephant, Sri Lankan elephant
European crow, Asian crow
Chinese goat, English goat.

We do use our reasoning power
not to find harmony
We take thrill in discordant notes
Love to split atoms
and destroy others
Human world is a rose flower
Each petal adds to its beauty
But when petals are nipped off
vanishes its splendour.

Part Two

Dear my fellow beings
why are we crazy of labels?
Western people, eastern people
white men, black men
Europeans, Asians
American, Africans
Indians, Chinese, Japanese
Germans, French, English
Australians, Canadians, Egyptians
Christians, Muslims
Hindus, Buddhists
Bengalese, Punjabis

Malayalees, Tamilans
Brahmins, Kshatriyas
Vaisyas, Sudras.

The Creator made no divisions
except man and woman
He made the division
to continue creation
In truth they are one
two sides of the flow

Part Three

Dear my fellow beings
there's no discrimination
of male or female in animal world
But look at the plight of female
in human world
Her birth is ill omen
Millions are butchered
before they are born
Parents receive her
as burden to family
She is destined to live
under her brother's shadows
Has to live on his leftover
She is denied good food
denied good dress
denied schooling
denied entertainments
Always jailed in kitchen
compelled to work
from dawn to midnight
None listens to her complaints
but tortures
if she opens her mouth
She has no choice
for her spouse
Often raped by her husband
He never cares
for her desires

Feeding of children
falls on her shoulders
Sacrifices her health
for entire family
Her struggle starts
from early morning
fights with utensils
in the kitchen
and then goes for
hazardous labour
till the dusk
She is born with a cry
goes on crying and crying
till she reaches
her destination death.

Woman is most venerable
for she is your mother
she is nurse and teacher
and above all
she is the lamp of house
Sexism is contemptible
A product of patriarchy
Patriarchy reigns supreme
in families, institutions
societies, nations
politics and religion
Woman is exploited everywhere
Religion aimed at ethics
discriminates her
Why can't women be priests
in churches, mosques and temples?
Can't she enter and pray
in her Heavenly Father's abode?

Man, woman is your counterpart
Why can't she be taken
as your own body?
Why is she viewed
as a consumer product?
Why do you look at her

with lascivious eyes?
Hasn't she right over her body?
Why do you dictate her apparel?
Why do you forget
that she is your mother
she is your wife
she is your sister
or she is your daughter?

Part Four

Dear my fellow human beings
be humble as all other beings
This planet is a home
to all objects living and non living
Kindly learn your position
You were born
as the youngest ones
All objects have
the right to exist here
You may live here
Let other things also live
Since you are selfish and greedy
you take more than
what is due to you
Other beings struggle for necessities
whereas you are after
comforts and luxuries
You become rich
pushing hundreds of your neighbours
to the abyss of starvation.

Part Five

Dear my fellow beings
though you are created a vegetarian
your greed for delicacies
extinguish other beings
Your greed for luxurious shelters
exterminate trees and forests

Your construction mania
defiles the sky and
topples the climate
You turn your villages to towns
and become more and more civilized
but less and less cultured
There was a time
when you loved
cohabitance with other beings
Cats, dogs, cows, goats,
fowls were your companions
Your civilization now
keeps them away
Your butcher culture
teaches you to kill them
and eat if edible
Your indiscriminate felling of trees
chased away all birds
Many have become extinct now
In place of cuckoos and nightingale
which lulled you to sleep
mosquitoes disturb your slumber
through injections and drone.

Part Six

Dear my fellow beings
you boast of your culture
you boast of your language
Is there any culture
which is not hybrid?
Is there any language
which is not mixed?
How many millions have been killed
in the name of culture?
Look into the pages of history
Most of the wars have been waged
for the supremacy of culture
Conquest of cultures over cultures
amalgamated to multicultural world
How much Indian is an Indian?

None can give any answer
Same who boasts of any nationality.

Part Seven

Dear my fellow beings
break away all fences and walls
Fences of your petty minds
Compound walls of your houses
Walls of your religions and castes
Boundaries of your native States
And ultimately borders of your nations
Let there be no India, Pakistan or China
America, Africa, Europe or Australia
But only one nation THE WORLD
where every being lives in perfect harmony
as one entity in multicultural world

Questions

- How are women glorified by the poet?
- What is the poet's view of purity of language and culture?
- How can multicultural harmony be achieved?

Siachen Tragedy*

Siachen glacier,
milky white grey hair of Himalaya.
Seventy kilometres long
and height ranging from
four thousand to six thousand metres
Twinkling by sun, moon and stars
Rarest beauty on earth for the heavens
Winter, winter, winter, forever and ever
Snowfall is thirty five feet
temperature minus fifty Celsius
Not a blade of grass grows
yet world's highest battlefield!
Thousands of soldiers of India and Pakistan
fight with Nature to secure their frontiers
Billions are spent for their outposts
Siachen glacier feeding several rivers
irrationally axed and dug
inviting vagaries of harmless Nature
Avalanche lodged on seventh April
buried hundred and twenty four soldiers
and eleven civilians under eighty feet snow
Isn't it high time the governments
stopped challenging benevolent Nature?

* The tragedy took place on 7 April 2012

Questions
- What is the Siachen tragedy?
- What is the message of the poem?

Horoscope

Horoscope, bread earner of astrologers
Arch-villain of Hindu marriages
Monster who pricked the rosy dreams
and sucked the blood of thousands of spinsters
An offspring of pseudoscience astrology
Man-made by-pass for 'happy' life
Christians and Muslims never follow
Are their lives worse than Hindus?
Do horoscopic matches bring happiness and peace?
Why then cases of thousands of divorces?
Peace and happiness are fruits of Karma
Horoscope is the product of religious mafia
A means to exploit laity's ignorance
Millions are trapped in this vicious circle
No sign of redemption in near future

Questions
- What is the poet's attitude to horoscope?

Global Warming's Real Culprits

America and other developed countries
stamp poverty stricken third world
and developing countries as
main culprits of global warming!
To them firewood and fossil-fuel gas
the arch villain of greenhouse gases
But thousands die every day
since smokes don't
emit from their kitchens
Billions survive each day
since such noxious gases
come out from their fireplace
Carbon dioxide produced by
home appliances of the rich
room heaters, air conditioners,
refrigerators, washing machines,
and the toxic emissions
from their cars and planes
plays the major share
in polluting air and
resultant global warming.

Questions

- Who are the real culprits of global warming, according to the poet?

Cohabitance on the Planet

Souls of the seven cats
Ammini, Manikutty, Preethi,
Kinganan, Kitty, Rowdy, Kittu
long for my lap and stroke
My neighbour dispatched
them in two years
Who says angels are in heaven?
They were all angels on earth
manifesting His beauty
exhibiting His Grace
to humans who
grope for Him in heaven
My neighbour believes
and millions believe
that He is in heaven
and He created the universe
for human welfare
that man is centre of creation
that he can dictate the planet
My neighbour believes
his wife is his own
his sons are his own
the mansion and compounds
are his own
all birds and animals on compounds
are his own
the earth and the air
are his own
He fails to learn
and millions fail to learn
that God is the sole owner
Empty handed we come
empty handed we go
We inhale what plants exhale
My neighbour disregards
and millions disregard
cohabitance with other beings
Souls of the seven cats

Haunt me and wound me
Unanimously they ask
why they were poisoned
Haven't they right to this planet?
Aren't they children of God?
Is it offence to run along the compound?
Is it sin to play hide and seek with birds?
Is it crime to defecate in pits
and bury it neatly?
Sweet memories of those pet cats
how they brought heaven to our house
torment us like thorns on our hearts
How can I avenge their deaths?
What law is there to punish my neighbour?
God, don't you hear their cries?
Don't you hear our cries?
I can only vision
my neighbour will be reborn
as a mouse to be chased
by half a dozen cats

Questions

- How does the poet vision his neighbour's rebirth?
- What is the message of the poem?

Multicultural Kerala

My native State Kerala
blessed with equable climate
and alluring landscape
crowned by the Sahyas
she lies on the lap of Arabian Sea
Multitudes of brooks and rivers
flow through her veins
Thousands of species of flora and fauna
Six months long rainy season
followed by summer bearable
Autumn and winter fear to enter
Tourists call it God's own country

Education makes one cultured and civilized
teaches one noble values and principles
Alas high rate of literacy
doesn't yield fruit to my fellowmen
They are puppets in the hands of
religious and political mafias
Become preys to superstitions,
offshoots of religious blind faith
Millions are spent for
senseless rituals and ceremonies

Education makes them crazy of
white-collared cosy jobs
Fertile arable lands and fields
lie like deserted wastelands
The State depends on neighbouring States
for food of all kinds,
Rice, wheat and other grains
vegetables, fruits, milk, egg, meat
Construction mania devours
paddy fields and arable lands
and defecate multi-storeyed structures
on mother-earth's lovely bosom
Educated youth of the State
not getting white-collared jobs

seek employment abroad
spending loans of lakhs from banks
What an irony! They are ready to do
hazardous laborious tasks
and even menial scavenger jobs

Kerala has become a haven
for North Indian labourers
Thousands flood to this heaven
and serve the indolent Keralites
Construction, agricultural, plantation
commercial, domestic and
such daily wage labours
go through their rocky hands
My State has thus become
cent percent dependent and multicultural!

Questions

- How has Kerala become a multicultural State?
- What trait of his fellow beings is attacked by the poet in this poem?

On Conservation

Hey poet, kindly heed to my plea
before you thrust your pen
into my bleeding heart
Though I am a passive sheet of paper
I have a soul as vibrant as yours
Please don't vomit your trash
through your volcanic missile
The less you write the more we live
the more our plant family lives
Kindly write on the need of the day
the necessity of conservation
of plants and animals on earth

Questions
- What is the plea of the sheet of paper to the poet?
- What is described as volcanic missile in the poem?

Charles Darwin, Patron Saint of Animals

Charles Darwin the great scientist
unravelled history of Creation
linked human beings with other beings
challenged pseudo religious claims
Religious fanatics injected
irrational theories and philosophies
to establish man's supremacy
and similarity to the Creator
"God created man in His own image!"
Isn't man more prone to vice than virtue?
How then has he God's image?
Do animals commit sins or crimes?
Hats off to Charles Darwin
the patron saint of other beings
Rational man will deem his
relation to the animal world,
respect their claims for coexistence

Questions

- Why does poet call Charles Darwin 'patron saint of animals'?
- Why does the poet say that man is not in the image of God?

Elephant Mania

Elephant the largest animal on earth
Famous for its memory and intelligence
But seldom knows its size or power
Hence cunning man enslaves it
Makes it dance to all his whims and fancies
Highly sensitive to heat
It's goaded along burning tar road
Speared often if it disobeys mahout
Forced to drag huge timber
Bear people on its back in tourist centres
An exhibit for temple festivals
Torture it with heavy sounds
of fireworks and drums
Unbearable it charges
on mahouts and crowd
How many have been killed thus?
Are gods crazy of elephants
or devotees elephant-maniacs?
Isn't it high time
we send them back to jungles
and thus save their lives and ours?

Questions

- How all are elephants tortured by human beings?

India, Number One!

Sixty percent of my countrymen
defecate in open place
Six hundred and twenty six million!
My country is number one in the world!
Dear my brothers and sisters abroad,
don't you see my country's growth?
Ninety seven percent of my countrymen
have no access to clean drinking water.
Yet the government claims
 the country is fast growing!
True, growth is there
in number of multi-millionaires
who are even less than two percent.

Questions

- In what respect is Indian number one, according to the poet?
- Wherein lies the growth of India, according to the poet?

Child Labour*

Dhanalakshmi, lass of eleven
Parents dreamt of making wealth
and named her thus
after the goddess of wealth
Her parents sick and poor
fail to feed their children
Crying hungry mouths
forced the wretched parents
to sell the eldest lass
With burning heart
and tears rolling down
the ma gave her parting kiss
Her trembling hands received
five thousand rupees
the price of her darling child
Reluctant and crying
Dhanalkshmi followed her master
Young and healthy Advocate
lived with his wife and children
Luxurious double-storied house
Dhanalakshmi cook-cum-maid
Her hellish life from dawn to midnight
Her tender soft palms
smooth as petals of lilies
burnt, bruised, bled
Sadist husband and wife
drunk and voluptuous
inflicted wounds on her body
Woke her up very early morning
burning her hand with cigarette ends
Starved her for sluggishness in work
Poor lass helpless and crying
None in the world
to share her sorrows
Longed for her parents call
to take her back home
Dreamt of a day
lying on her ma's lap

caressed by the loving hands
When children of her age
strolled gaily to their schools
tears ran like brooks
Tired of overnight's late labour
couldn't fall in for duty at dawn
The monster mistress poured
hot water on her sleeping head
Poor lass shrieked with deadly pain
The neighbours swarmed to the house
hearing this piercing scream
Took the child to the nearby hospital
showering abusive words
on her master and mistress
Phoned to the police
and got them arrested
The channels flashed the news
Millions prayed mute
for Dhanalakshmi's precious life
And alas she left the world
immersing the whole state
in an ocean of grief and wrath

* The tragedy took place in February 2011

Questions
- What happened to Dhanalakshmi?
- Why was Dhanalakshmi sold by her parents?

Caste Lunatics

Prakash Jaatav, aged thirty one
riding on his motorcycle
attacked by a group of twelve
beat him and slashed his nose
The reason for this diabolic act?
"The Dalits have no right to ride motorbikes
in presence of high caste men."
My country, the greatest democracy,
when will it be freed from
lunatics of caste and religion?

*The incident took place in Madhya Pradesh, India reported by NDTV on 12th June 2012.

Questions
- What is the theme of the poem?
- What happened to Prakash Jaatav?

Bulbuls' Nest

My jasmine plant
with myriads of hands
embraced the slender pole
Entangled like a
lass's dishevelled hair
Sprinkled with flowers
sparkling like stars
Allured a pair of
red whiskered bulbuls
Intoxicated by fragrance
started building a nest
Their sweet high note music
echoed our house and compounds
God has sent them
recompense for our
murdered seven cats
Delightedly we watched
every step of their architecture
We tried our best
not to frighten
our divine guests
Neither were they
 scared of the hosts
Ten days of incessant work
magnificent nest was ready
Two purple eggs then
Hatching for twelve days
Started feeding the nestlings
Guests of four in our outhouse
We were extra vigilant
to scare off covetous crows
The guests may leave us
after a fortnight
Still that heavenly bliss
happiness for ever

Alarmed by their shrieking wail
we dashed towards the jasmine

A rat snake close to the nest
Frightened, climbed down
and sped its way
Alas, the chicks were swallowed!
Wretched bulbuls
wailed for two days
and disappeared for ever
My wife still disagrees
for letting the snake go elated
I have never seen it
before or after
Isn't He who sent it
as the bulbuls were?
How can a host
ill-treat a guest?
He who creates
destroys as well.

Questions

- Explain the lines "He who creates / destroys as well."
- Make note of the nature description in the poem.

Beena's Shattered Dreams*

Unbearable to look at
their darling daughter's still body
parents fell unconscious
Beena's corpse was brought from Mumbai
accompanied by her roommates.

Her parents made her nursing graduate
taking loans of lakhs from bank
and spending from their meagre daily wages
What all dreams were there for her,
her parents and her younger sister!

The Mumbai Hospital had offered her
monthly salary of thirteen thousand,
free food, boarding and travel
She had to live in cell in hostel
with three other colleagues
Had to cook her meals
Had to spend fifty rupees daily
for rickshaws taking her to the hospital
She was paid only nine thousand
and had to work more than twelve hours a day
and that too with an irregular schedule

She wanted to escape from that hellish world
longed to return home
and seek a job in a better hospital
But authorities won't let her go
unless fifty thousand paid
for breach of contract
They can violate all agreements
and none is there to question them
No law is there to punish them
Alas, dreams and hopes being shattered,
losing strength to face all challenges,
Beena bade adieu ending her life

The three estates of my great country
and the fourth estate too,
the largest democracy in the world!
Don't you listen to the wails and sobs
stormed from Beena's writhing parents?
Have you lost your conscience
witnessing thousands of Beenas every day?

* The tragedy occurred in October 2011

Questions
- What was Beena's dream and how was it shattered?
- What canker of the State is pictured in the poem?

Mullaperiyar Dam*

A dam aged hundred and sixteen,
built without cement but surkhi and lime,
blocking innocent frisky Periyar,
immersing millions of plants and trees,
fleeing thousands of animals and birds.
It postures now Janus-faced;
its old age worsened by frequent tremors,
head to foot bleeding in several parts,
makes millions tense and sleepless on one side.
Catastrophic fear culminated to
behavioural problems in children nearby;
daren't go to school, neither parents dare to send;
anxiety, phobia, depression, insomnia!
If broken, forty millions in five districts affected.
People in unison clamour for new dam:
"Give them water and save our lives."
Millions on other side object to new dam;
Disbelieve promise of water from other side.
Arid five districts made fertile using the water.
Political mafia beguiles innocent masses
People on both sides lived as one family
Alas! Anti-social forces injected
regional, racial venom in masses;
destroy farms, attack shops and buses.
Multitudes flee to their native villages
leaving whatever they have earned with sweat.
Borders are closed, police patrol,
Inter-state buses and trucks stop run;
fruits, vegetables and eggs are rotten;
thousands of farmers, labours and merchants
struggle for their daily lives.
Rulers of State and central governments
living in midst of pomp and luxury
heed not to the wails and moans of the masses.
Avarice for power obstructs their duties;
tests the patience of benevolent Nature
and leaves the masses preys to calamities.

*The poem is composed based on newspaper reports during monsoon in 2011.

Questions
- What is the issue of Mullaperiyar dam?
- What is the poet's complaint against State and central governments?

I Wish I could Fly Back

I wish I could sit on Time's shoulder
and fly back to my youth
I could then be jolly
with my friends and colleagues
who bathed me with pure love
which flowed from their surging hearts
I do have friends today
who are selfish, fake and fraud

I could then sit my daughter and son
on my lap to shower them with warm kisses
Carry them on my shoulder
and listen to their jingling babble
I could watch their nimble feet
moving like musical notes
They both are grown up now
making my lips dry and droughty

I could then love my ma more
help her in her domestic works
make her happy with sweet loving words
caress her hands and feet when lying tired
buy her new dress on carnival days
How little I could return her
when compared to her tsunami of love!
Alas I can only long for
as she has flown to her Father's abode

Questions
- Why does the poet wish to fly back?
- What does the poet wish to do if he could go back to his mother?

Pearl's Harbour*

Parents who christened her 'Pearl'
never dreamt her becoming real pearl
A real gem to hundreds of desolates
Pearl aged thirty one
and her only daughter Kalinga
living with seven other kids
and mothers two—all forlorn
Living with a mission in life
No mother shall sell her child
complying to Hunger's call
No mother shall kill her child
for being born of illegal father
Her rented house at Alappuzha**
a bower of love and benevolence
Born to wealthy parents
postgraduate in Social Work
married to Prasanth an industrialist
Truly made for each other
both were humane and philanthropists
Helped orphans and wretched
from profits of their business
Alas Creator called him back
through a car accident
Pearl fulfilled Prasanth's dream
'Pink' was formed for charity
Returns from his business partnerships
flow as milk and food
to hundreds of forlorn mouths
Unlike Rossetti's Blessed Damozel
he never yearns for Pearl's reunion
Pearl is a role model
to thousands of wealthy parents
who luxuriate in their mansions
with a child or two and servants plenty

*Based on the newspaper report in *The Mathrubhumi* on 20 April 2011
**A coastal town in Kerala, India

Questions
- What is Pearl's mission in life?
- How did Pearl's house become a harbour?

Dignity of Labour

Imitating the Whites
fashionable to the Blacks
particularly to my countrymen
Mimic dress, hairstyle
food, drinks and all
such sensory pleasures
My countrymen fail to imitate
noble qualities:
industry, perseverance,
enterprise, adventure,
equality, fraternity,
cleanliness, health
love of nature
and environment
Laziness is their chief trait
Agricultural labourers,
sweepers, scavengers,
fishermen, tailors,
barbers, drivers
and all such workers
who serve the mankind
often underdogs
and seldom deemed
Parasite politicians
bogus sanyasis and clergies
white-collar bureaucrats,
corrupt and inefficient,
models and heroes
and honoured by my society!

Questions
- What according to the poet is the chief trait of his countrymen?
- What are the noble qualities which the poet's countrymen fail to imitate?

Drowned Dreams*

Shijin Das and Jibin
friends aged eighteen
students who passed intermediate
wanted to serve the country
and earn their livelihood
Preparation for naval recruitment
wanted to learn swimming
tried in flooded paddy field
Their bubbles of dreams pricked off
sinking their parents and dear ones
in tears they were drowned
Bharat Matha,
why didn't you hold them from sinking
who were willing to guard you from enemies?

*Based on a tragedy that took place at Enavoor, Kerala, India on 12 June 2012.

Questions

- What was the dream of Shijin Das and Jibin and how was it drowned?
- How apt is the title of the poem?

Hungry Mouths

"My sweet son,
finish your rice;
why so slow?"
"Ma, enough for me;
can't eat any more."
"Ouch! Why took so much
and made such waste?
Dear, you don't realize
the price of your leavings;
it can save
a child like you
from his death today.
Thousands of children
are famished
in our country
and other countries
day after day.
Leftovers of the
ten percent Haves
can sustain
ninety percent Havenots
and make this hellish world
a blissful heaven.
My dear child
whenever you
sit before food
lend your ears
to the hungry cries
of millions of kids
and the moans
of their helpless mummies."
"Very very sorry ma
I will never waste
any food in future.
Ma, we shall keep
a portion of our food
and send it to
those hungry mouths."

"Right my child,
we will do
what we can do
to silence those wails."

Questions

- What is the message of the poem?
- What decision have the mother and child taken at the end of the poem?

Ananthu and the Wretched Kite*

Ananthukrishna, God's innocent child
confronts with a kite, God's own dear creation
No reason for spite or revenge
Little lad is chased by the kite
pecks him on head and back
on his journey to school and home
Compelled to go with parent and umbrella

A fortnight ago some elder naughty boys
pelted stones at the wretched kite
Even wounded by a stone on its back
Boys fled away leaving Ananthu alone
Poor kite mistook him as assailant

Accipitrine birds like kites, hawks, eagles,
God created them carnivores
Prey on birds, insects, animals for survival
Whereas we human beings
butcher animal world
not for existence but for taste
Nocturnal birds like bats and owls
ominous for us human beings

When will we begin to love
 kites, eagles, bats, owls
as we long for parrots, cuckoos,
skylarks and nightingales?
When will we stop the massacre
of animals, birds and fish
and learn to respect
other beings and their right to live?
Based on newspaper report

Questions
- Why does the kite attack Ananthu?
- What is the message of the poem?

A Spider in My Bathroom

A spider in my bathroom
To smite or spare?
Lives on mosquitoes
who inject me
The creator has sent
it along with mosquitoes
Being a poet vowed
to love all creations
what shall I do?

Questions
- What is the dilemma of the poet?

Fruit of Labour

Mr. Mony, my painter,
deserted by money itself
Tightened his belt
to sustain his family
Had to live in a rented hut
with his unemployed wife
and two little lads

Mony led a team of dozen
frisked with colours and brushes
Bathed houses, schools,
colleges, churches, hospitals,
offices, monasteries
and sky scrapers
with dazzling, delightful colours,
and filled eyes and minds
of his employers
with immense joy and happiness

Mony started his career
with a meagre wage of fifty
A humble breakfast at ten
was his lone diet during duty
When he painted my house once,
his teammates went to dine
during lunch break
But he was sitting on the veranda
with a beedi burning on his lips
"Mony, why don't you go for lunch?"
"Sir, I am not used to lunch.
How can I spend more
from the fifty rupees I get?"
Right, Mony went on painting
from little rooms to steeples,
nurturing colourful dreams
of a house of his own one day
and government jobs to his children
Sons were sent for professional education,

taking burdensome loans from banks

Mony's days have come at last!
Goddess of wealth has descended
to his humble house
Both his sons are employed with high salary
Are married to brides with fine income
Have bought a house and cars two
Mony, my painter, is really happy now
He goes on painting with his colleagues
gets reasonable wage of five hundred
He dances with his brush and colours!
But never goes to take his lunch
his only luxury a drink in the evening

Questions
- What was the fruit of labour painter Mony got?
- What is the message of the poem?

Sail of Life

My morning walk takes me
to a tea stall
The lone opened shop
at the still Gandhi Square

I am astonished
by the din and bustle
that comes out
from all opened stalls
in the evenings

My boisterous sail will reach
its harbour one day
I will be astonished
by its stillness and darkness

Questions
- Bring out the imagery and symbolism used in the poem.

Valueless Education

Shocking news shrieked newspaper readers
Fourteen year old tenth class Legin*
fiendishly murdered by his classmate
A year old grudge of the culprit
Revenge for a blow from the victim
Invited friendly to the school urinal
Stabbed several times on chest and neck
Hacked off head with a knife
Then cracked it with a large rock
Torn whole body with a piece of glass
Left the corpse with little grief or remorse

Where does our education
lead teenage minds to?
The young culprit leads a discontent life
Lives with his mother,
Deserted by his father
who lives with his fourth wife
Gets no value from his home or school
Visual media leads him astray
Becomes fan of Rambo films
Worships fictitious hero
who can kill all enemies
He too keeps a knife in his socks
and a glass piece wrapped in kerchief

Media, print and visual
forget ethics they are bound to follow
Instead of being a correcting force
to all subjects and other estates
filling minds with eternal noble values
they inject venoms of violence
communalism and superstitions
They focus terrorists and anti heroes
Arch corrupters and human deities
And no wonder, tender minds
are bewitched by their illusion

*The heinous crime took place in St. George's Higher Secondary School, Muttar, Kerala, India on 7th May 2012

Questions
- What is the theme of the poem?
- Why does the poet criticize media?

Musings on My Shoes

Dear my black leather shoes,
I should prostrate over you
for carrying seventy kilos
for more than two years
You are relieved only
a few hours at nights
Yet how little did I
deem your service!
You lifted me from
dust, mud and all such filth
Seldom did I heed to your
terrible tearful travail:
the way man slaughtered you
to extract your hide
Off my feet I threw you
out of my vicinity,
displeased with the stench
excreted from my feet
How can one be crueller than this?
How ungrateful I have been!

Same is the plight of proletariat
They are shoes worn by the rich
Service being complete
they are spat out like curry leaves
Women too are often treated like shoes
Mothers and wives when old and weak
Become burden to sons and husbands

Question

- How does the poet compare shoes' service to proletariat and women?

Multilingual Black Drongo

Black Drongo the black beauty
Proud of its diverse sounds and tails
Homo sapiens feel proud
of its speech and language
Other beings can't follow it
Same is the case
with non-human sounds
Which scientist can read
cries of animals and birds?
Black Drongo speaks
in more than seven sounds
Even imitates cat's sound
And its species reads them well
and responds sweetly.
How sweet and musical
are the sounds of animal world
when compared to the toxic sounds
vomited by the human species
defiling air chaste and pure!

Questions

- What difference does the poet find in animals' language and human's language?

Mukesh's Destiny*

Poor parents named him Mukesh
Perhaps longed their son
to be great like legendary singer
or multibillionaire Ambani
Born to impoverished Dalit parents
studies in fifth standard
Fate defies him at this tender age
Mother bed-ridden with mouth cancer
Compelled to forgo all treatment
Father, the bread earner
fell victim to acute asthma
Little Mukesh is their lone support
Works in nearby estates
on all holidays and even working days
When his classmates enjoy holidays
his nimble feet and soft hands
clash with rough tools and hard earth
How can government turn face to
Mukesh and his wretched parents?

*Based on the news report in the Malayalam daily *The Mathrubhumi* on 30 June 2012.

Questions
- What is the destiny of Mukesh?
- Who is responsible for the child labour of Mukesh?

Lottery Tickets Sellers

Blind old man
weak and bony
leaning on staff
holding lottery tickets
in tremulous left hand
His lone dependent
and supporter as well
spouse old and weak
through whom
he knows the world
leads him by hand
to the queue of men
waiting at the liquor shop
Another blind youth
pocketed with tickets
stationed at entrance of
chief government office
Similar sight of a ticket seller
a youth who has lost
both his hands
pleads for commuters' mercy
in buses after buses
with tickets and money
hanging in two pockets
They all try to bring
fortune to their customers
Alas, goddess of fortune
never cares for them

Question
- What is the irony of the lives of lottery ticket sellers?

Mahi's Fourth Birthday*

Mahi's fourth birthday
clad in new gaudy dress
celebrating with her friends
playing near the house at 11pm
fell into that hellish trap,
a deserted uncapped bore well
seventy feet deep
Poor kid's faint wails added by
shrieking cries of her parents,
friends and relatives
Rescue operation led by army,
supported by fire force,
police, tunnelling experts,
officials of health, revenue, security,
a team of more than hundred
worked hard for long eighty six hours,
digging parallel well nearby,
while two thousand million minds
bled with deep anguish
and their prayers soared high
for the little angel's life
Alas, the army personnel brought out
decomposed body of Mahi
She died of asphyxia
within three or four hours,
the post-mortem revealed
Envious of the poor child's happiness
gods in heaven dragged her there
to entertain them with her mirth
Innocent children fall victims
to careless adults' negligence
and the culprits go acquitted

* The tragic incident occurred at Manesar Village in Haryana, India on 20th June 2012.

Questions
- What happened to Mahi on his fourth birthday?
- Who is responsible for Mahi's tragedy?

Who am I?

"Who are you?" my superego asked
"I am Prof. K. V. Dominic, MA, M.Phil, PhD," my id replied
"Alright, what else?"
"English poet, short story writer, critic, editor."
"Keep that long tail under your armpit," superego exploded.
"An illiterate farmer is greater than you;
His service is greater than your scribbling;
Labourers' sweat is dearer than your ink;
If they strike, your writings will cease,
and ultimately you yourself will disappear.
Hence support them and write on them;
Proclaim to the world the noble
service they render to the humanity."

Questions

- What is the theme of the poem?
- Why should we support farmers and labourers?

Bathroom Monologues

Bathroom
A cell one loves deep
One which gives most relief
Both physical and mental
A place of countless monologues
Muses descend there
Orpheus opens your lips
Music flows from you
to the accompaniment of
rhythmic sounds of shower
There you are the monarch
No complexes rein you
You sing to your content
The birth of ideal creativity!

Question
- Why does the poet say that ideal creativity is born in bathrooms?

Martyrs at the Borders

Chilly freezing Line of Control
Two Indian soldiers shot dead
by Pakistan counterparts
A body even beheaded and mutilated
Similar accusations from Pakistan soldiers
Precious human lives little value there
Values frozen with passionless life at high altitude
When billions of compatriots
live peacefully with their families
on either sides of LoC
thousands of soldiers patrol day and night
deprived of warmth of love
from their spouses and children
How their families long to meet them
counting down months and days!
How these guardian angels
thirst for communion with their families!
How much of a country's revenue
allotted for its defence every year!
Total money spent on defence
can wipe out poverty from the planet for ever
Is human species so belligerent and destructive?
Aren't the masses peace lovers,
benevolent and compassionate?
Why then such a huge waste
for defence unnecessary?
Why create tension at the borders?
A means to divert subjects' attention
and muffle mass' protest against corruption?

Questions
- What is the theme and message of the poem?
- Who are actually the warmongers, people of a country or their rulers?

Mother's Love

Maternal love, love sublime
Inexplicable, unfathomable
Noblest of all emotions
Visible both on human beings
and other beings
Both on domestic animals
and wild animals
Mother feeding babies
seeking food for them
with much labour
She eats only after
they are fed or
leaving portions for them

Maternal love is transcendent emotion
Both human species
and other species possess
I am perplexed
by some sporadic disasters
A mother offering her
affectionate daughter
to please her lover's sexual urge
How could she throw her dear child
to the hungry wolf?
How could she suppress
the divine emotion of maternal love?

Questions
- Why is mother's love called noblest of all emotions?

Tears of a World Champion*

Kudos to Indian Blind Cricket team
2012 World Champion
Hats off to Mr. A. Manish
Middle order batsman and fine fielder
A role model to people with eyes
Resurrected like a phoenix bird

Lost eyesight at the infant age of three
Thatched hut of the family
burnt very close to him
Helpless baby went on crying
till the hut turned to ashes
Instead of tears puss flowed
from eyes next morning
Lost one eye's function cent percent

Father died after six months
Mother sent him to Blinds' School
Studied till higher secondary
The school could find his cricket talents
Got selected into Kerala State team
And later into Indian team
And now world champion at 24

But his jubilations can't last long
Has to regain mason work
at the mixing company nearby
Has been doing so for several years
to earn bread for him
and his depending family
Has got three sisters
and one has to be married off

Manish yearns for government's mercy
A permanent job
as reward for his service to nation

   * Based on newspaper report

Questions
- Why is the world champion in tears?
- How did Manish lose his eyesight?

Thodupuzha Municipal Park

Municipal park at Thodupuzha
beckons me my evenings
A haven for the townsmen
fleeing from their burning houses
Afternoon heat of thirty eight degrees
Sweating throughout due to humidity
Why to blame sun or gods?
Man has dug his grave
Not only his but other beings
and the planet itself

Though not vast, an ideal park
Full of trees and river adjacent
Symphony of the chirpings from above
Rustling of gentle breeze on leaves
Mixed sounds of flowing vehicles

Seated on a concrete bench
my senses feast beauties one by one
Little kids on swings and merry-go-rounds
captivate my eyes and mind
Little ones of all creations
eternal beauties that haunt our minds
Those little kids' merry pendulum swings
pull me back to childhood days
How much I longed for a swing
made of ropes and coconut leaf!
How I fell once rope broken
How ma beat me for swinging and falling

Those parents pushing kids on next swing
nostalgically draws my mind
to our occasional visit here a score year back
myself, Anne and our little two kids
How much we enjoyed from their happy swings!

Gone are those happy days with little kids
They have grown up and flown away from us
Anxiety of their future welfare has replaced
peace and happiness that haunted in our house

Question

- What nostalgic feelings and thoughts pass through the mind of the poet when he visits the park?

Why is Fate So Cruel to the Poor?*

Latehar District in Jharkhand
One of the poorest in 'fast growing' India
Landlessness and graft in public schemes
compel the villagers every year
to migrate to neighbouring Bihar
for a few months
to work on landowners' vast farms
in exchange for paddy grains
No wages but one by twelfth of the harvest
That too deducting the food they ate
The rate remains the same
even after long eight years
Exploitations questioned by none
None to protect the wretched
Not even the One who created them
Eighth January 2013
The blackest day for the unfortunates
The hired truck carrying sacks of grains they earned
Workers sitting on the top of the sacks
tried to protect them and the children
from the bitter chill of the night
Alas! The truck swerved and overturned
Twenty five labourers and ten children
died suffocated under heavy sacks
They struggled hard for the grain
and the grain led them to their graves
Why is fate so cruel to the poor?

   * Based on newspaper report

Questions
- What fate of the poor people is described in the poem?
- Bring out the irony in the lines "They struggled hard for the grain / and the grain led them to their graves."

Women's Cricket World Cup 2013

I.C.C. Women's Cricket World Cup 2013
Played in cricket crazy land of India
Opening match at Brabourne ground, Mumbai
Indian lasses meeting West Indian lasses
Live telecast from Star Cricket
What a shame! Empty galleries!
Had it been men's world cup
galleries full and thousands ticketless outside
Why such discrimination to women's sports?
Why such double standards to women's feats?
Had it been women's beauty contest
or fashion show with minimum dress
the stadium would be full
even if tickets are very high
Dear my brothers in India and abroad
let's appreciate and promote
our sisters' talents and skills
rather than looking at them
with vicious hungry eyes.

Question
- What is the poet's plea to brothers in India and abroad?

ACTS–Saviors on the Roads*

ACTS: Accident Care and Transport Service
Founded at Thrissur, Kerala in 1999
More than thirty thousand voluntary helpers now
Doctors, engineers, teachers, daily wage labourers
Fourteen branches, fourteen ambulances
Free service in the entire district
Flown to more than fifty thousand accident spots
Taken more than a lakh bleeding lives to hospitals
Thousands of bruised dead bodies
to police stations and mortuaries
ACTS has become the culture of the land
Ethos of a humane enlightened people
Sensing others agony as one's own
Finding time for others
even in one's busy hectic life

* Based on newspaper report

Question
- What is ACTS and how do they serve the society?

Beach Beauticians*

Kozhikode beach in Kerala
Beautified by four beauticians
Salih and his three mates
Free voluntary service
from six to eight all morning
When others enjoy morning walk
they get greater happiness
in serving them and
thousands who frequent in evenings
Bought brooms, baskets, spades, pickaxes
Start cleaning from one end
removing garbage, plastic,
grass and mud on road sides
setting loosened tiles in position
Ten days to reach the other end
and then another ten on return
Role models to the human race
Treat public place as our own compounds

* Based on newspaper report

Question
- How do Salih and his friends beautify the beach?

A Tribute to Sakuntala Devi*

7,686,369,774,870 x 2,465,099,745,779
The answer in just twenty eight seconds!
= 18,947,668,177,995,426,462,773,730
Guinness Book Record in 1982
Kudos to Sakuntala Devi, the "Human Computer"
Born to a trapeze, tightrope performer
having no formal education
surprised all as mental calculator
from the tender age of three
University scientists bowed their heads
amazed at her skill at age of six
23rd root of 201-digit number
she could answer in fifty seconds!
Cube root of 188138517
she could do it faster than a computer
Marvel to the East and the West
her loss is literally irreplaceable
Praise to the Almighty
for His revelation through a human brain!

* Shakuntala Devi was an Indian writer and mental calculator from Bangalore popularly known as "human computer." She died on 21 April 2013.

Questions
1. Why is Shankuntala Devi called a human computer?
2. What is her Guinness Book Record?

Celebration of Girl-Child's Birth*

The greatest celebration of girl-child's birth
the highest model to the entire world
The slaughterhouse world where thousands
of female foetus are killed everyday
Piplantri villagers in Indian State Rajasthan
angels on earth creating a paradise
A girl-child's birth celebration to the entire village
Earth, sky, trees, flowers, rivers, birds, flies
welcome the newcomer dancing
Hundred and eleven saplings
brought by women to newborn's house
They are to be planted in the village
and nurtured throughout their lives
The villagers collect twenty one thousand rupees
donate to newborn's father
Adding his own ten thousand
deposits in child's account
a fixed deposit for twenty years
The child shall get maximum education
Not married before maturity
The noble practice started in 2007
The village head Shyam Sundar Palival
started this exemplary project
A memorial of his departed girl child
The village is now blessed with
two lakh fifty thousand robust trees
Fruit trees and herbal trees
Their leaves and fruits yield
great income to the villagers

*Based on *The Mathrubhumi* report on 5 June 2013—the World Environment Day.

Question
- How do Pipalantri villagers celebrate girl-child's birth?

Where shall I Flee from This Fretful Land?

Once God's own country with equable climate
Rainy season for six months
and mild summer for the rest of the year
Blessed with brooks, rivers, lakes and greeneries
Now people crazy for material pleasures and luxuries
tumbled nature's balance and bounties
resulting scanty rain and intolerable heat
So where shall I flee from this fretful land?

Once fertile land for free and secular thoughts
People lived in multicultural harmony
Hindus, Muslims, Christians lived as brothers and sisters
respected each other and their religious views
Now hell of intolerance and religious fundamentalism
So where shall I flee from this fretful land?

Once politicians were apostles
Their selfless service to the nation
lauded gratefully by the people
Now people look at them with dubious eyes
for corruption is stamped on their brow
National income created of sweated labour
looted by these ignoble lazy cheats
So where shall I flee from this fretful land?

Question
- Why does the poet want to flee from his land?

Homage to Swami Vivekananda*

Swami Vivekananda,
the morning star of the East
The magnetic seer with his
reasonable rendition of religion
Religion as scientific as science
Religion is science of consciousness
Religion is universal experience
of transcendent Reality
Science and religion complementary
He freed religion
from the hold of superstitions
Freed it from dogmatism
priestcraft and intolerance
Religion is pursuit of supreme Freedom
Supreme Knowledge and supreme Happiness
He laid foundation for spiritual humanism
which makes life meaningful and worth living
He taught world man should be pure
for purity is our real nature and soul
We should love and serve our neighbours
for we are all one in the Supreme Spirit
.
India's greatest cultural ambassador to the West
taught his countrymen
how to master Western science
based on Indian spirituality
How to adapt Western humanism
to Indian life and culture

* World Celebrated Swami Vivekananda's 150th Birthday on 12 January 2014

Questions
- What is Vivekananda's view of religion?
- Why is Vivekananda called the cultural ambassador of India?

Agitation through Farming*

Arippa land agitation
Thousand two hundred landless families
agitating for land past one year
Converted eight acre wasteland to rich farm land
Yielded rich harvest of vegetables
and more than forty quintals paddy
Sold in open market as 'Arippa Fresh' rice
Tapioca grown in seven acres

Agitation under Adivasi Dalit Munnetta Samithi
Encroached fifty six acres of surplus rubber estate
acquired by the State government
Protesters ranging from ninety year old
to two-week infant live in shanties
more than thousand erected on the estate
They don't misappropriate estate assets
but demand land as means of livelihood
and for roof over their heads
They have spread a strong message
Unassessed government lands lying idle
could be used for feeding hungry mouths

*Based on the report in *The Hindu* on 8 January 2014. Arippa is a place in Kollam District, Kerala, India

Question
- What message do the land agitators spread?

An Ideal Festival*

Annual festival of Chittanjoor St. Mary's Orthodox Church
A role model to festivals of all religions
Originally planned for grand festivity
Though church of Christians, Christians few in number
It's church of Christians, Hindus and Muslims

Atul Krishan a youth of eighteen
Son of house opposite to church
Died of bike accident a week ago
Fr. Pathrose summoned festival committee
Committee comprising mainly non Christians
Made his suggestion to cancel festivities
When a family of mother and sister mourning
how can there be happiness and merriment?
The committee agreed unanimously
Cancelled booking of elephants and bands
Celebrated festival with just a Holy Rasa
Erected a tall stone lamp with the money collected
The community prayed for the soul's eternal rest

* *Chittanjoor St. Mary's Orthodox Church is in Thrissur District, Kerala, India. Based on Malayala Manorama report on 2 January 2014*

Question
- How did the Church festival become an ideal one?

Protest against Sand Mafia*

New Delhi's Jantar Mantar
Haven of Satyagraha strikers
Thirty one year old Jazeera
with her three little kids
The youngest boy only two
Tented on the footpath
Staying on a cot under plastic sheet
Neither torrid heat of summer
nor freezing cold of winter
can defeat her will power
Protest against sand mafia
looting thousands of tones
from northern beaches of Kerala
Huts of poor labourers
swallowed by sea one by one
Police and government helpless
Jazeera's protest goes on for six months

Does she miss the warmth of home?
Is she guilty about her children?
What about their schooling?
Will her protest go unnoticed?
Her honest answer is
"I am doing this for my children
If we don't stop them now
there'll be nothing left on the beaches
Our houses will submerge in the sea."
For whom is the government?
Law-breakers and criminals or their victims?

*Based on the report in The Hindu on 9 January 2014

Question
- How did Jazeera protest against sand mafia?

Synopsis

Multicultural Symphony is Prof. K. V. Dominic's third collection of poems after *Winged Reason* (2010) and *Write Son, Write* (2011). Having set a style of his own, Prof. Dominic writes on contemporary burning issues and topics in Wordsworthian lucidity and simplicity of expression. Imagination gives way to Reason in his poetry, and for him content or message is more important than the embellishments. Written in free verse, each of his poems makes the reader contemplate on intellectual, philosophical, spiritual, political, social and environmental issues of the present world. There are forty seven poems in this collection on a variety of topics ranging from multiculturalism, global warming, conservation, horoscope, casteism, dignity of labour, child labour, poverty, unemployment, environmental issues to purely subjective introspective matters.

A Collection of New Poems

Previously unpublished works of
K.V. Dominic

Contents
Book 4 -- A Collection of New Poems

An Airport Made of Tears* 220

Brahman's Leela 222

Child Trafficking 223

Flower Vendor 225

Haiku 226

I can Hear the Groan of Mother Earth 228

Karma is Akarma 229

Mahadeva Prasad, Saviour of Deserted Girls* 230

Maternal Attachment 231

Mother India, I Weep... 233

Murugan, God of Beggars* 235

Nadarajan, the Ideal Neighbour* 237

Parental Duty 238

Parents Deserted 239

Servants Assume Masters 240

Shinu's Marathon for Charity* 241

Tribute to Siachen Martyrs 242

Vasudhaiva Kutumbakam 244

Venkatachalam, Saviour of the Old* 246

What is Karma? 247

Salute to Farmers! 249

Evolution Of A Poem: Tribute to Siachen Martyrs 251

Untitled (1st Draft) 252

Tribute to Siachen Martyrs (2nd Draft) 253

Goa Outreach: Helping Street and Slum Children in India 255

An Airport Made of Tears*

Proposed Aranmula International Airport
A dream project of private construction group
Intends to construct airport city in 3000 acres
Eighty percent land paddy fields and wet lands
Rice and fish can earn four hundred crores per year
Runway being constructed over tributary of Pamba
Will lead to flood in river during monsoon
Razing of four hills for filling wet lands
Leading to water shortage and loss of biodiversity
Will affect serenity and sanctity of Parthasarathy temple
Three thousand poor families to be evicted
But they are not willing to leave
their sustaining lands, jobs and houses

Fake development policy of the State
Dancing to tunes of billionaire corporate
An airport totally unnecessary
Two international airports on either side
Two hours drive will take you there
Selfish discontent inhumane millionaires
Insist on flying from the poor's chest
Got sanction from Sate through foul means
Already filled hundreds of acres of paddy fields
Destroyed hundreds of species of fish, snakes,
amphibians, valuable plants and micro-organisms
Fled thousands of birds both air and water

Aranmula people are on indefinite satyagraha
Protest against merciless State and corporate
Young and old they clamour in unison
"We will never leave our houses and lands
Where will we go and how will we live?
We can't leave our rich heritage village,
our Parthasarathy temple and holy groves
Let their armed force shoot us all
and construct airport over our corpses."
Their elected government has betrayed them
The government pleads for the corporate

Ignores the pleas of opposition parties
Pooh-poohs warnings of environmentalists
Innocent villagers lulled by music of birds and hymns
Waken up again by heavenly symphony
And eased by gentle strokes of breeze in day time
are destined to bear day and night
piercing drones of planes one after other

Beware, Maoists are never born
They are made where injustice rules

*Arnamula is a Hindu heritage village in southern part of Kerala. The place is internationally known for Parthasarathy Temple, Holy Snake Boats and boat race, Aranmula Mirror and holy river Pamba.

The poem was composed on 28 February 2014 and recited at the main auditorium of Pondicherry Central University on 20th March 2014 before leading English poets, writers and professors from all parts of the country.

Questions

- Why does the poet oppose Aranmula Airport project?
- Why does the poet call the State's development policy as fake?

Brahman's Leela

Every thing comes out of nothing
And goes back again to nothing
And this cycle goes on
Started from time immemorial
And continues eternal
All Brahman's Leela
Brahman full of perfections
Hence no purpose in creation
Nothing to be obtained by creation
Spontaneous creation of universe
Leela, Leela, Brahman's blissful sport
Precipitates pain as well as joy
He who learns it, least affected
Has neither joy nor sorrow
Remains in heaven on earth

Questions

- What started from time immemorial?
- Why is Brahman's (Creator) activities called a Leela or blissful sport?

Child Trafficking

National Crime Records Bureau's
distressing, shocking revelation:
A child just disappear overnight
every eight minutes!
Children taken from their homes
and sold in markets
just like cows or goats!
Sold for bonded labour!
Amputated, blinded,
defaced with acid for begging!
Sexual exploitation
from the tender age of five!
Young girls made sex slaves
and forced prostitution!
Organs of children sold
and earn thousands!
Kidnapped children and
those sold by their parents!
Abject poverty compels parents
to leave their darlings
with bleeding hearts
and shaking hands!
Traffickers beguile them
with hollow promises
Believe their kids are driven
to secure happy homes
Forty thousand children
abducted in India every year!
Twelve thousand women
and fifty thousand children
trafficked for sex trade from
neighbouring countries every year!
India bears three lakh child beggars!
Forty four thousand children
fall into gangs' clutches every year!
How can man be cruel like this!
Non-human beings always
love their offspring and

protect them from all dangers
Human being refined being
proves often debased being!

Questions

- What tragic face of India is depicted in the poem?
- Explain the last lines of the poem "Human being refined being / proves often debased being!"

Flower Vendor

Flower vendor Soundira Rajan
Surrounded by flowers of dozen varieties
Rose, marigold, dahlia, daffodil,
jasmine, chrysanthemum, daisy, tulip
Dawn to night intoxicated by fragrance
Eyes bathed in alluring colours
Those pretty tempting flowers
Nature's bounties for human minds
Balm for burning minds young and old
stimuli for amorous outburst
But unwelcome guests for Soundira Rajan
Jasmine garlands he makes for brides
remind him painfully of his unmarried daughter
Still remains single at thirty two
Arch villain dowry stands as stumbling block
Wreaths he makes with trembling hands
reminiscent of his spouse bed-ridden with cancer

Questions
- Why are the flowers unwelcome guests for the flower vendor Soundira Rajan?
- What do jasmine flowers remind Soundira Rajan?

Haiku

Jackfruit longs for mellow:
can serve as feast
to birds and squirrels

Teachers shunned by students:
couldn't serve as models
and conquer their minds

Rains reluctant to descend:
no shrubs and trees
to welcome their arrival

Elephants kill mahouts:
man has no right
to torture them

Children become obese:
artificial hormonal food
and lack of physical exercise

Tigers enter villages:
how will they survive
when forests are encroached?

Twinkling stars remind human beings
Smile, weep not, SLEEP
Learn from non human beings

Stray dogs multiply:
Beastly man throws away
offsprings of pets on roads

Cauliflowers weep:
bathed in insecticides
flies don't kiss them

Why didn't wash your dish, daughter?
If mama could do it,
why can't you then, dear papa?

Cattle thank God:
their traffics on trucks are blocked
Gluttons of beef weep

Infant's innocent smile:
Smiles at nothing
Finds beauty everywhere

Questions
1. Why are rains reluctant to descend?
2. What do twinkling stars remind human beings?

I can Hear the Groan of Mother Earth

I can hear the groan of mother earth
being raped by her own beloved human sons
Having sucked all milk from her mountain breasts
quarry deep out of construction mania

I can hear her shriek for help
when they cut each her vein
and drain all brooks and rivers

Can't you hear your mother's wail
when they pluck her hair after hair
felling trees and plants which protect them?

I can hear the scream of elephants, tigers,
Boars, snakes and all wild animals
when they drive them from their homes
and starve to death by burning forests

I can hear the death cry of bird after bird
when they cut their feeding trees
to make their selfish life more luxurious

Man, can't you hear those tremors of curses
hurled on you by endangered animals, birds and plants?
Man, I can hear mother earth cursing you
As Gandhari did long back to Lord Krishna

Questions
- Why does mother earth groan?
- Why do the wild animals scream?

Karma is Akarma

Karma has Akarma
Akarma has Karma
One who knows it
Reigns kingdom of wisdom
He alone does real Karmas
Karma belongs to senses
Senses part of Prakruti
Atma does no Karma
Hence Karma is Akarma

Notes:
    Karma means action, work or deed
    Akarma means inaction
    Prakruti means "nature" or "primal motive force."
    Atma means mind, soul, spirit or psyche

Question

- How does Karma become Akarma?

Mahadeva Prasad, Saviour of Deserted Girls*

Sukrutam Gardens
deserted girls haven
Twenty five abandoned inmates
between six and seventeen
Mahadeva Prasad bachelor of forty
their father and brother
Managing trustee of Sukrutam
Started this shelter in rented house
Later bought 2.5 acres at Kozhikode
selling his family share
and built a house in it
getting help from his friends
Organized trustee with his friends
Girls studying in various schools
Prasad would try his best
to get them employed
and married off to loving husbands
Udaya, a trustee member
is their caring loving mother
Coming back from schools
they do farming in their compound
or learn lessons of cooking
Elder ones take care younger ones
They are no more orphans
Sukrutham is no doubt
a home of love and happiness

*Based on *The Mathrubhumi* report on 18 May 2014.

Question
- How does Mahadeva Prasad prove himself as a saviour of deserted girls?

Maternal Attachment

Who can measure mother's immaculate love?
He can measure quantity of oceanic water
He can number the stars on blue sky
How much a mother lives for her child!
How much she pains and grieves for her offspring!
How much she bore carrying him/her in womb!
How much a mother sacrifices for her baby!
For feeding it her milk several times a day
how much she sacrifices controlling her food!
How she spends her sleepless nights
feeding and rocking when it goes crying and crying!
When mothers burn out thus for their babies
fathers lead a less tense tiresome life
Lesser time they spend with newborn babies
I feel guilt of learning this too late for recompense
How much my mother loved and lived for me!
How much she grieved, pained, fed, worked,
even starved and spent sleepless nights
watching eagerly each my movement
savouring gaily my growth day after day
From zero I have grown to this stature
I want to express ma my gratitude
Just to give her a kiss on her forehead
as return for her thousands of kisses
Alas! She left me five years back
not waiting for any returns from me
Compared to my wife's pains and struggles
nourishing my daughter and son in infancy
mine were negligibly less
They both are grown up now
and daughter has become a mother
Still my wife's sufferings continue
Her sleepless nights have come back
caring daughter and child with pleasure
while I sleep cosy unperturbed by infant's cry
How shall I define mother's love?
No lexicon term can convey it
Inexpressible, indefinable, unfathomable

immaculate, eternal and divine is maternal love!

Questions

- How does the poet define mother's love?
- Explain the line "I feel guilt of learning this too late for recompense".

Mother India, I Weep...

Mother India, you used to get up
full of vigour and thrill
roused by Sun your God
But angered by your ungrateful sons
He wakes you now with sweating rays
Trees, forests, hills,
rivers, lakes and wet lands
bathed you in refreshing rain
Maintained healthy temperature
Your wicked sons shaved off
plants and trees that cooled your body
Where are those mounds and hills?
Where are those wet lands and fields?
They levelled to build skyscrapers
and overburden you like Atlas
Seeing you lamenting helplessly
Mother India, I weep...

We used to wake up greeted by
music of birds like crows and cuckoos
Nature's hymns at dawn to the Creator
Gone are those birds and music now
Dins from temples, churches and mosques
Hymns to gods who never demand
Gods are pleased by karmas alone
Sattvic karmas, which your children seldom do
Hours wasted on rituals and rites
Then engaged in tamasic, rajasic karmas
Seeing our people's incorrigible actions
Mother India, I weep...

When you were enslaved by
foreign kings and empires
Looted your wealth and
trampled exemplary culture
Your valiant sons and daughters
fought against them
shedding their blood and

even sacrificing their lives
For them love of motherland
was the first and foremost feeling
Your plight is worse now Mother
Your politician sons suck your blood
Rape you and even attempt matricide
They shoot arrows and you lie bleeding
Unlike Bhishma lying on bed of arrows
could choose time of his death
you are dying inch by inch day after day
Most of your children are weak and helpless
to resist these villains' heinous assault
Seeing you writhing and crying for help
Mother India, I weep...

Questions

- Why is Mother India lamenting?
- What are the incorrigible actions of the people which make the poet weep?
- Who is Bhishma?

Murugan, God of Beggars*

Nothing gives greater happiness
than living for the poor
Prophets' lives are examples
Murugan, youth at Kochi city
aided by his MBA wife
lives for beggars and the wretched
Picks them day after day
from streets in his auto rickshaw
Shelters them in his own made one room hut
Bitter childhood, father plantation labourer
Deserted jobless mother and children
Family shifted to city slums
Murugan fought with dogs
for kitchen garbage from hotels
Br. Mavurus took him
to Don Bosco children's home
Stayed there for eight years
Learned to read and write
Coming out to street again
struggled for sustenance
Did all kinds of menial jobs
Determined to save his people
Made an organization for tramps
The first in the world
for vagrants on streets
Br. Mavurus funded him
for his one room shelter and auto rickshaw
Could save five thousand beggars
lepers, lunatics, drunkards, bed-ridden,
deserted mothers, blinded, amputated kids
Sought meanings to their tortured lives
Got President's award for his divine service
True, Murugan reigns as God in hundreds' minds

*Based on the report in *The Mathrubhumi* on 11 May 2014

Question
- How has Murugan become God of beggars?

Nadarajan, the Ideal Neighbour*

Nadarajan aged seventy two
staying in a hut of polythene sheet
in Pothupara village of Konni Taluk in Kerala
Ekes out living by sharpening kitchen knives
Lone fighter against granite quarry mafia
which grabbed neighbouring lands
menacing people of quarry's dangers
Nadarajan determined to save the village
and never to yield to mafia's threats
Decided to distribute his fifty cents
among ten poor landless families
The Western Ghats Protection Council
identified ten beneficiaries
on request from benevolent Nadarajan
Nadarajan's exalted exemplary action
is the real Karma which can motivate
in the thickly populated exploited State

*Based on the news report in *The Hindu* on 16 June 2014

Question
- How has Nadarajan proved an ideal neighbour?

Parental Duty

What right have parents on their children?
What right has man on this universe?
Are we the cause of the existence?
This flow has started time immemorial
Aren't we just bubbles of that great flow?
You can't rein the flow of the system
But simply flow like an autumn leaf
Why then concern too much of your offspring?
Never dig your grave as Dhritarashtra did
Best is to be models to your children
Leading lives of dharma and karma

Question
- What according to the poet is the parental duty?

Parents Deserted

Stunned by reports in newspapers
Parents in eighties and nineties
needing bed rest and medication
admitted in hospitals by children
When asked to pay medicine bills
desert them and disappear for ever
Some are dropped on roadsides
Some even in thick forests
lonesome and prey for wild animals
How can offspring be so ungrateful!
Bore them for nine months in womb
Breastfed for a year or more
Turned blood to sweat and even starving
nurtured with food, clothes and education
Sought hard for their employment
Found suitable partners for their marriage
Looked after their tots
when they went for work
Old and weak when such parents
need support from their children
how can they be treated as burden?
How can they be spat out like curry leaves?
Deserting them is like selling cattle
when they are old and useless
to the slaughterhouses of Kerala
Beware! Life is a vicious cycle
Today's children tomorrow's parents!

Question
- Why are the parents compared by the poet to cattle?

Servants Assume Masters

In democratic government
people are masters and
bureaucrats servants
Applicants and petitioners
ought to be welcome
seated and requested
"What shall I do for you Sir/Madam?"
But what happens in our country
shames us and startles world
Masters request servants
"Sir, what shall I do for you?"
It's our curse here
bribes and graft rule service

Question

- What is that in India shames the countrymen and startle the world?

Shinu's Marathon for Charity*

Eighth marathon for bachelor Shinu
A humanitarian youth of twenty eight
A vegetable vendor from Trivandrum
Not a contest for any trophy
Solo race for charity fund raise
Twenty three children and
sixty grownups wait for his return
Their treatment and survival
depend on the money he earns
Already earned and spent
twenty two lakh rupees for
sixty patients last seven years
Crossing seven districts
he has entered now Idukki district
His target is six lakh rupees
"None be denied treatment
due to lack of money," he says
Souls like Shinu are the saving
grace of this inhumane world
who props it from eternal doom

*Based on the report in *The Mathrubhumi* on 31 July 2014

Questions
- What for does Shinu run marathon?

Tribute to Siachen Martyrs

What a heart-bleeding eye-flooding
scene on the front page of newspaper!
Four month old daughter Meenakshi
shown her father's frozen dead body!
Lance Naik B. Sudheesh meeting
his darling lone daughter for the first time!
Alas neither of them identifies each other!
What a depressing sobbing sight for mass assembled!
Tsunami of groans, laments, weeps and sighs!
Youth of twenty nine, Sudheesh had planned
to visit home on leave after a month
Could come a month before immersing all in tears!
Married Shalu, degree student three years back
Thus sacrificed his life for the nation along with
nine others in Siachen Glacier at Indo-Pak border
Were buried under thirty feet huge avalanche
Bodies could be recovered only after seven days
Thousands are still patrolling there
ready to die for their nation any moment
Siachen Glacier highest battle field on earth
Twenty thousand feet above sea level
Lowest temperature minus fifty degree
Average winter snowfall thousand cubic meters
Nothing lives there except Indo-Pak soldiers
Indian army controls area since 1984
More than two thousand soldiers
sacrificed precious lives for India and Pakistan
When hundred and fifty crores people
cosily sleep with family in both the countries
Thousands of young lives are compelled to leave their family
to fight with merciless climate for no reason or gain
When thousands die of hunger everyday on either side
hundreds of millions are spent on this vulnerable place
Whose craze it is? For whom it is? People's welfare?
People aren't iron-hearted to see their patriots
suffer so sorely and sacrifice their precious lives
Let dove of peace fly over Indo-Pak borders
nay, borders of each and every nation

God, kindly sow seeds of peace, love and
compassion in the minds of all nations' heads

Questions
- Explain the line "Alas neither of them identifies each other!"
- What is the message of the poem?

Vasudhaiva Kutumbakam

Laws of Vasudhaiva Kutumbakam
eternal laws of the planet
Meant for humans and non humans
But rational human beings never care
Violators everywhere
and abiding very few
No government to enforce laws
All animals have fellow feelings
Carnivores prey not for thrill
but for existence
But man kills man not for food
Intelligence makes him narrow
His irrational divisions of classes--
colour, caste, religion,
language, politics, nation
demote love and promote hate
When millions die of hunger
trillions spent for armaments
Selfish thirst for comforts and luxuries
devastated ecology and
flow of the system
When we eat our food
cooked in our kitchen or
bought from supermarkets
we never think of that star
one fifty millions kilometres away
showering light and energy
on plants which feed us
as well as animals on earth
Human world always dependent of
plant world and animal world
Extinction of any species
 affects our own survival
Damages done to ecology
can't be remedied singular
Needs collective efforts of nations
Let's hence abide by the eternal
laws of Vasudhaiva Kutumbakam

Questions
- What is meant by *Vasudhaiva Kutumbakam*?
- What are the eternal laws of *Vasudhaiva Kutumbakam*?

Venkatachalam, Saviour of the Old*

Fed up of your old parents who
fed you till they became old and week?
Nuisance for your cosy privacy life?
Want to dispose them like old cattle
but afraid of legal consequences?
You may call Mr. Venkatachalam
the home nurse who showers love
and selfless service on old and deserted
Nearing sixty he has completed
silver jubilee of 24x7 service
Going from patients to patients
homes to homes and towns to towns
Seldom visits his own wife and children
Parents deserted, starved and tortured
by their own blood born selfish children
take him as their loving son
and he consoles them back
when they weep and wail
"Aren't I with you always?"
He feeds them, bathes them,
sits by them day and night
Lulls them by the songs they like
and finally helps them
enter their Father's abode peacefully
Venkatachalam sets an example
to new gen cut throat children
how to be humane to their loving parents

* based on the newspaper report in the *Mathrubhumi* on 27 July 2014

Questions
- How does Venkatachalam serve as Saviour of the Old?
- What is the message of the poem?

What is Karma?

"What is Karma?"
Joseph, youth of twenty
asked his parish priest, Fr. Francis.
"Great question!" Fr. Francis answered.
"When one learns its answers
and applies it on life
becomes wise and jnani.
Our Indian philosophy
richest mine of any such riddle.
Three types of karmas:
Tamasik, Rajasik, Satvik."
"Kindly explain, Father."
"Speech and deeds not caring result,
minding not feelings and emotions,
just like the action of a terrorist
is Tamasik, which you shall never do.
Words and actions
done to please oneself
fall under selfish Rajasik karma.
Words and deeds
done to serve others
are selfless Satvik karma
which makes you a saint."
"How can one be Satvik, Father,
when Greed is chasing like a monster?"
"Tapas can drive any Greed;
need not go to the Himalayas;
meditation in one's room is enough.
Satvik karma bears no stamp of the doer;
it's purified action emitted like a ray.
Once done the doer shall never remember;
never expect return from beneficiary;
not even grateful words or look.
Satvik person overcomes emotions;
negative emotions of anger, apathy,
conceit, despair, doubt, envy,
fear, greed, guilt and hate,
never dare enter one's mind.

Loves all objects of universe;
animate and inanimate;
animal world and plant world.
Learns the truth 'aham brahmasmi'
'I am the infinite reality.'
Thus attains realization of life."
Fr. Francis enlightened Joseph's mind.
"Thanks a lot Father for
showing me the right path."

Questions

- What is Satvik Karma?
- Differentiate between Tamasik and Rajasik Karmas.
- What does aham brahmasmi mean?

Salute to Farmers!

Farming, noblest of all calling
Most terrestrial and natural
Innocent human beings beckoned
by mother earth to dig out
treasures from her infinite chest
Farmers gently hunt out using
spades, ploughs, harrows etc.
Wicked mafia sons suck her blood
Inject venoms to her veins
and even rape her to death
How pleasurable farming is!
Getting up early morning
farmers are allured by plants
just like their own children
Their eyes are bathed in happiness
when they find plants' growth
leaf after leaf and flower after flower
and fruit after fruit getting to ripen
Their eyes are drowned in tears
when they find beloved plants
withered or dead by bad weather
Farmers, feeders of a nation
less remembered gratefully
or least honoured and rewarded
Always praying for the mercy of God
Risking drought and flood
they have only tales of tears
Outcome of their sweat
looted by the mafias
and they starve and cultivate
to feed the nation's parasites
Numbers of their suicides
increase year after year
Let's salute our farmers for they
are the backbones of our nation

Evolution of a Poem: Tribute to Siachen Martyrs

The idea of writing a poem on the death of 10 Indian soldiers by avalanche at Siachen Glacier at Indo-Pak borders originated in me on 3rd February 2016 the very day of the tragedy. The sad news of it flashed in TV and a very detailed one in the newspapers the next day. How to begin and how to end and what all ideas are to be included—those were my thoughts during my one hour morning walks on the following days.

Thus after a week I started to type it on my desktop computer. I never write with pen nowadays, but only directly typing the matter on the desktop as to save my time. Given below is the original draft without any title. The title was fixed and given at the second draft which is the final one as well. I have shown in the final draft with **<u>boldface underline</u>** the changes I have made to the first one.

Untitled (1st Draft)

What a heart bleeding tear flowing
Scene on the front page of newspaper!
Four month old daughter Meenakshi
Shown her father's frozen dead body!
Lance Naik B. Sudheesh meeting
His darling lone daughter for the first time
Alas Neither of them knows each other!
Meenakshi not old enough to know her dad
Lifeless eyes of Sudheesh can't see his offspring
Aged twenty nine Sudheesh planned
To visit home on leave after a month
Could come a month before immersing all in tears
Married Shalu degree student three years back
Thus sacrificed his life for the nation along with
Nine others in Siachen Glacier at Indo-Pak border
Buried under thirty feet huge avalanche
Bodies could only be recovered after seven days
Siachen highest war front in the world
Nineteen thousand feet above sea level
Lowest temperature minus fifty degree
Average winter snowfall thousand cubic meters
Nothing lives there except Indo-Pak soldiers
Indian army controls area since 1984
More than two thousand soldiers
Sacrificed precious lives for India and Pakistan
When hundred and fifty crores people
Cosily sleep in both the countries
Thousands of young lives are compelled
to fight with merciless climate for no reason
when thousands die of hunger everyday on either side
hundreds millions spent on this vulnerable place
whose craze it is? For whom it is? People's welfare?
People aren't iron-hearted to see their patriots
Suffer so sorely and sacrifice their precious lives

Tribute to Siachen Martyrs (2nd Draft)

What a heart-bleeding <u>eye-flooding</u>
scene on the front page of newspaper!
Four month old daughter Meenakshi
shown her father's frozen dead body!
Lance Naik B. Sudheesh meeting
his darling lone daughter for the first time!
Alas neither of them identifies each other!
<u>What a depressing sobbing sight for mass assembled!</u>
<u>Tsunami of groans, laments, weeps and sighs!</u>
<u>Youth of</u> twenty nine Sudheesh **<u>had</u>** planned
To visit home on leave after a month
Could come a month before immersing all in tears!
Married Shalu, degree student three years back
Thus sacrificed his life for the nation along with
nine others in Siachen Glacier at Indo-Pak border
<u>Were buried</u> under thirty feet huge avalanche
Bodies **<u>could be recovered only</u>** after seven days
<u>Thousands are still patrolling there</u>
<u>ready to die for their nation any moment</u>
<u>Siachen Glacier highest battle field on earth</u>
Twenty thousand feet above sea level
Lowest temperature minus fifty degree
Average winter snowfall thousand cubic meters
Nothing lives there except Indo-Pak soldiers
Indian army controls area since 1984
More than two thousand soldiers
sacrificed precious lives for India and Pakistan
When hundred and fifty crores people
cosily sleep **<u>with family in both</u>** the countries
Thousands of young lives **<u>are compelled to leave their family</u>**
to fight with merciless climate for no reason **<u>or gain</u>**
When thousands die of hunger everyday on either side
hundreds of millions are spent on this vulnerable place
Whose craze it is? For whom it is? People's welfare?
People aren't iron-hearted to see their patriots
suffer so sorely and sacrifice their precious lives
<u>Let dove of peace fly over Indo-Pak borders</u>
<u>nay, borders of each and every nation</u>

<u>God, kindly sow seeds of peace, love and compassion in the minds of all nations' heads</u>

Goa Outreach:
Helping Street and Slum Children in India

Goa Outreach is a small project helping local disadvantaged children regardless of their religion, class, caste or gender. Many of these children are slum and street children who have arrived in Goa alone or with their families from neighbouring states in the hope of an easier and better life. Many children end up working on the streets to support the family income, this is often in the form of Rag Picking with children, usually in small groups, walking around the streets picking up items which are later sold at recycling centres. Other children can be found working the beaches begging, selling trinkets or other small items.

Goa Outreach provides a route into full-time education by accessing schools for the children and providing support to encourage them to stay in school on a regular basis. The support includes uniforms, books, bags, footwear, fees and other requirements and of course keeping a check on their performance and attendance.

Health is another important role as the children we help often suffer from long-term health problems, treatment for which is not always available early on and slum conditions may well exacerbate these problems. Scabies, impetigo, conjunctivitis are common issues that are easily spread with burns and infected mosquito bites often going untreated resulting in more severe infections leaving scars as well as the danger of contracting Malaria or Dengue Fever.

To help the children with health care we provide free medicines and pay for any hospital or doctors fees. In addition to this, we also give out monthly health packs to promote cleanliness. Mosquito protection is also given to families as Malaria, and other vector borne diseases are a threat to families living in the slums.

We want to be able to give street and slum children a chance of a childhood worth remembering. We want them to study hard, but we also want to provide them with a safe and fun environment with access to toys and games which other children take for granted.

With this in mind, we created Goa Outreach. Please check out our blogs which are updated monthly.

www.GoaOutreach.org

Index

A Blissful Voyage, 5
A Cow on the Lane, 97, 98
A Nightmare, 6
A Sheep's Wail, 8
A Spider in My Bathroom, 184
A Tribute to Sakuntala Devi, 208
ACTS--Saviors on the Roads, 206
Agitation through Farming, 212
aham brahmasmi, 248
Ahimsa, xvi
Akarma, 229
Ammini's Demise, 47
Ammini's Lament, 46
An Airport Made of Tears, 220
An Elegy on My Ma, 89
An Ideal Festival, 213
Anand's Lot, 10
Ananthu and the Wretched Kite, 183
Ananthukrishna, 183
Antharjanam, C., 108
Aranmula International Airport, 220
Arippa, 212
Arnamula, 221
Ashwatthama, 129
Atma, 229
Attachment, 100
Aung San Suu Kyi—Asia's Lady Mandela, 102
Bathroom Monologues, 197
Beach Beauticians, 207
Beauty, 12
Beena's Shattered Dreams, 172
Beevi, R., 108
Bhai, D., 123
Bhishma, 234
Black Drongo, 191

Brabourne, 205
Brahman's Leela, 222
Bravo Katie Sportz!, 103
Bulbuls' Nest, 170
Caste Lunatics, 169
cats, 136
Celebration of Girl-Child's Birth, 209
Charles Darwin, Patron Saint of Animals, 164
Child Labour, 167
Child Trafficking, 223
Chittanjoor, 213
City Versus Village, 54
Coconut Palm, 104
Cohabitance on the Planet, 159
Connubial Bliss, 13
Crow, the Black Beauty, 105
Cry of my Child, 55
Cuckoo Singing, 14
Darwin, xix, 143, 164
Dhanalakshmi, 167
Dhritarashtra, 238
Dignity of Labour, 179
Don Bosco, 235
Drowned Dreams, 180
Elephant Mania, 165
Enavoor, Kerala, 180
Evolution of a Poem, 251
Favitha, 98
Flower Vendor, 225
Flowers' Greetings, 106
For the Glory of God, 108
Fruit of Labour, 185
Gandhi Square, 187
Gayatri's Solitude, 15
GIEWEC, 140
Gill, S., xvi, 60

Global Warming's Real Culprits, 158
Goa Outreach, 255
God is Helpless, 110
Haiku, 226
Harvest Feast, 19
Haves and Have-nots, 20
Helen and her World, 22
Homage to Swami Vivekananda, 211
Horoscope, 157
How I Became a Vegetarian, 57
Human Brain, 43
Hunger's Call, 112
Hungry Mouths, 181
I am Just a Mango Tree, 24
I can Hear the Groan of Mother Earth, 228
I Wish I could Fly Back, 176
IAF Vayu Shakti 2010, 113
IJML, 140
In Memoriam George Joson, 1
In the Name of God, 52
India, Number One!, 166
Indian Democracy, 44
International Women's Day, 26
Jaatav, P., 169
Jantar Mantar, 214
Joseph, T. J., 127
Joson, G., xvii, 1
Karma is Akarma, 229
Kaumudi Teacher is no More, 56
Kcherry, S., 68, 147
Konni Taluk, 237
Kozhikode beach, 207
Krishna, 128, 228
Lal Salaam to Labourers, 28
Latehar District, 204
Lawrence, D.H., 12
Laxmi's Plea, 30
Leela, 219, 222
Line of Control, 198
Lines Composed from Thodupuzha River's Bridge, 138
Long Live E. K. Nayanar, 3
Lottery Tickets Sellers, 193
Madhya Pradesh, 169
Mahadeva Prasad, Saviour of Deserted Girls, 230
Mahapatra, J., xv
Mahi's Fourth Birthday, 194
Manesar Village, 194
Manish, A., 200
Martyrs at the Borders, 198
Massacre of Cats, 94
Maternal Attachment, 231
Mavurus, 235
Michael Jackson, King of Kings, 58
Mony, 185
mother earth, 71, 228, 249
Mother India, I Weep..., 233
Mother's Love, 199
Mukesh's Destiny, 192
Mukhopadhyay, A., 139
Mullaperiyar Dam, 174
Multicultural Harmony, 149–55
Multicultural Kerala, 161
Multilingual Black Drongo, 191
Murugan, God of Beggars, 235
Musings from an Infant's Face, 115
Musings on My Shoes, 190
My Teenage Hobby, 32
Nadarajan, the Ideal Neighbour, 237
Nature Weeps, 117
Nature's Bounties, 33
Nayanar, E.K., 3
Old Age, 35
Om, 49
On Conservation, 163
Onam, 37

Pamba, 220, 221
Parental Duty, 238
Parents Deserted, 239
Parthasarathy temple, 220
Pearl's Harbour, 177
Periyar, 174
Pleasures and Pains, 51
Pothupara, 237
Prakruti, 229
Prem, PCK, 69–73
Protest against Sand Mafia, 214
Rafi, M., 130
Rahul's World, 39
Resolution, 120
Rocketing Growth of India!, 121
Rocky, 136
Sahya, 138, 161
Sail of Life, 187
Sakuntala Devi, 208
Salute to Farmers, 249
Saraswathi, 130
Satvik karma, 247
Satvik Karma, 248
Satyagraha, 214
Servants Assume Masters, 240
Shijin Das, 180
Shinu's Marathon for Charity, 241
Siachen Glacier, 242, 251, 252, 253
Siachen Tragedy, 156
Singh, R.K., 139
Sister Mercy, 123
Sleepless Nights, 40
Solar Eclipse, 50
Soundira Rajan, 225
Sportz, K., 103
St. George's Higher Secondary School,, 189

Sukrutam Gardens, 230
Sukrutham, 230
Swami Vivekananda, 144, 146, 211
Tears of a World Champion, 200
Teresa's Tears, 124
Thodupuzha Municipal Park, 202
Thodupuzha River, 138
Thrissur, Kerala, 206
To My Colleague, 126
To My Deceased Cats, 136
Train Blast, 128
Tribute of Mohammed Rafi, 130
Tribute to Siachen Martyrs, 242
Tsunami Camps, 17
Valueless Education, 188
Vasudhaiva Kutumbakam, 244
Venkatachalam, 246
Victory to thee, Mother India, 92
Vrinda, 41
Wagamon, 131
Water, Water, Everywhere…, 133
What a Birth!, 42
What is Karma, 247
Where shall I Flee from This Fretful Land?, 210
Who am I?, 196
Why is Fate So Cruel to the Poor?, 204
Wolfgang, the Messiah of Nature, 135
Women's Cricket World Cup 2013, 205
Wordsworth, xviii
World Water Day, 133
Write My Son, Write, 74–88

Inside one of Contemporary India's most Influential Poets

The 24 papers in *Philosophical Musings for a Meaningful Life* study the poetry collections *Winged Reason* (2010), *Write Son, Write* (2011), and *Multicultural Symphony* (2014), of Dr. K.V. Dominic and reveal his humanistic values and concept of universal brotherhood, his social criticism devoid of absurdity and obscurity, his profound concern for the marginalized sections of society, and his reverence for Nature.

All the papers focus on the poet's anguish at the evils and the inhuman attitude prevalent in the society and necessitate harmony of existence. In the context of Indian English poetry, the papers find Dominic to be unique in his use of simple and plain language to address the vast canvass of human life and the neglected segment of human society. Further, the papers bring out how the universal appeal of Dominic lies in his ability to view the world as a sanctuary and acknowledge him as the promising voice of the present century for his belief in the interrelatedness of all lives that ascertains positive change in the individuals.

"This critical study on the poetry of Dr. K.V. Dominic deserves to be read closely for evaluation and to be on the shelf of every notable library. *Philosophical Musings for a Meaningful Life* will inspire scholars from the West to find rubies and diamonds in the Indian poetry of today."

--Dr. Stephen Gill, Poet Laureate of Ansted University

From the World Voices Series
Modern History Press
www.ModernHistoryPress.com

International Journal on Multicultural Literature

International Journal on Multicultural Literature (IJML) is a peer-reviewed research journal in English literature published from Thodupuzha, Kerala, India. The publisher and editor is Prof. Dr. K. V. Dominic, renowned English language poet, critic, short story writer and editor who has to his credit 27 books. He is also the secretary of Guild of Indian English Writers, Editors and Critics (GIEWEC). Since 2010, IJML is a biannual journal published in January and July. The articles are sent first to the referees by the editor and only if they accept, the papers will be published. Although based in India, each issue includes worldwide contributors.

Although IJML concentrates on multiculturalism, it also encompasses other literature. Each issue also includes poems, short stories, review articles, book reviews, interviews, general essays etc. under separate sections. IJML is available in paperback, Kindle, ePub, and PDF editions.

International Journal on Multicultural Literature
A Refereed Biannual published in January and July
ISSN 2231-6248

Available from Amazon.com, EBSCOhost, and other academic literature distributors

For more information or to subscribe, please visit
www.profKVdominic.com

Write My Son, Write
Text and Interpretation
An Exercise in Close Reading

Dr. Ramesh Chandra Mukhopadhyaya

"Write My Son, Write" is K. V. Dominic's longest poem, in 21 sections taken from his collection of poems entitled *Write Son, Write*. Dominic unabashedly tackles everyday issues of India such as the social injustice of poverty, man's crass exploitation of natural resources that ought to belong to everyone, terrorism, and the eternal beauty of the natural world. This poem is the manifesto of Dominic's views and philosophies.

K.V. Dominic writes, "People today are crazy after materialism, and divinity in them is being lost to such an extent that they give no importance to principles, values, family and social relations, cohabitance with human beings and other beings. Instead they are trying their maximum to exploit their fellow beings, other beings and the planet itself. If it goes like this, the total destruction is not far away. It is the duty of the religious leaders, political leaders and the intelligentsia to inject the lost values to the masses and thus preserve this planet and the inhabitants from the imminent devastation. Instead, majority of these leaders become mafias and inject communal and corruptive venom to the minds of the masses. Corruption has become the hallmark of these leaders and influenced by them the masses also deviate from the right track to the evil track. And who will save this society? Writers, particularly poets who are like prophets."

Dr. Ramesh Chandra Mukhopadhyaya's commentary provides the most complete critical analysis of the poem, section-by-section and line-by-line. Born in 1947, Ramesh Chandra Mukhopadhyaya M A (Triple) MPhil, PhD is a retired college teacher now residing in Howrah, West Bengal, India. A Bilingual writer (English and Bengali), he has been writing on different subjects for the last thirty years. He seeks to retrieve the wealth of poetry when it is a revelation.

Dr. Mukhopadhyaya regards K. V. Dominic as a poet of a seer.

From the World Voices Series
Modern History Press
www.ModernHistoryPress.com

**Modern History Press Presents
Diverse Voices from South Asia**

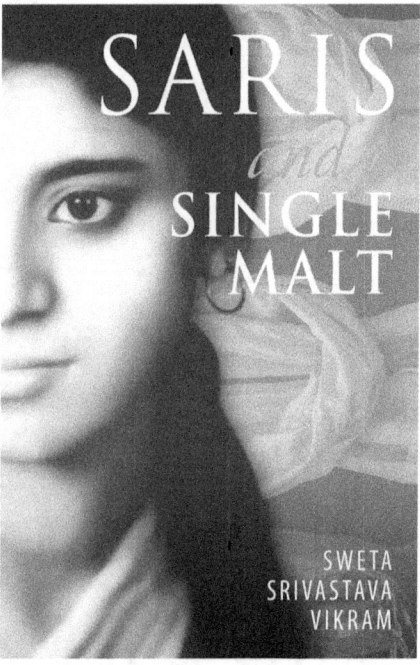

www.ingramcontent.com/pod-product-compliance
Lightning Source LLC
Chambersburg PA
CBHW052104230426
43671CB00011B/1932